连士升

（1907年5月24日—1973年7月9日）

  连士升是新加坡和马来西亚上世纪五六十年代的著名华文作家。他生于中国福建省福安县（1989年已升为福安市）。上中学以前，他熟读古代经典，奠定了良好的文史学问基础。1931年他从北京燕京大学经济系毕业后，留在北京从事经济史学术研究和著述。三十至四十年代，受战乱影响，他颠沛流离，但仍创造机会研究、写作、翻译和办学。1948年他受聘于新加坡《南洋商报》，在该报当特派记者、主笔、编辑、总编辑，直至1971年退休。

  连士升文笔精练，文章富有哲理。他悲天悯人，坚毅朴实的性格，自然地流露于字里行间。他著作丰富，2011年北京大学出版社收集他的著作，出版了《连士升文集》。该文集共五卷。第一卷为四本游记，第二卷为四本散文，第三卷为四本传记，第四和第五卷为八本《海滨寄简》。

  除了写作，连士升也积极推动艺术、文化、教育等社会活动。他曾任新加坡南洋大学筹备委员会委员，新加坡大学理事会委员，南洋学会会长，中国学会副会长，新加坡政府公共服务委员会委员。为了表彰他的贡献，新加坡政府于1963年授予他公共服务纪念奖章。

[新加坡] 连士升 著

给新青年
For the New Youth

洪婉玲　林展熠　译

北京大学出版社
PEKING UNIVERSITY PRESS

图书在版编目(CIP)数据

给新青年 /（新加坡）连士升著；洪婉玲，林展熠译. —北京：北京大学出版社，2019.8

ISBN 978-7-301-29958-6

I.①给… II.①连… ②洪… ③林… III.①青年修养 IV.①B825.4

中国版本图书馆CIP数据核字(2018)第 231165 号

书　　　名	给新青年 GEI XIN QINGNIAN
著作责任者	[新加坡] 连士升　著 洪婉玲　林展熠　译
责任编辑	王禾雨　任蕾
标准书号	ISBN 978-7-301-29958-6
出版发行	北京大学出版社
地　　　址	北京市海淀区成府路 205 号　100871
网　　　址	http://www.pup.cn　新浪微博：@北京大学出版社
电子信箱	zpup@pup.cn
电　　　话	邮购部 010-62752015　发行部 010-62750672 编辑部 010-62752028
印　刷　者	涿州市星河印刷有限公司
经　销　者	新华书店
	880 毫米 × 1230 毫米　32开本　6.75印张　191千字 2019 年 8 月第 1 版　2019 年 8 月第 1 次印刷
定　　　价	38.00元

未经许可，不得以任何方式复制或抄袭本书之部分或全部内容。
版权所有，侵权必究
举报电话：010-62752024　电子信箱：fd@pup.pku.edu.cn
图书如有印装质量问题，请与出版部联系，电话：010-62756370

前　言

　　1953年的夏天，我和内子及亮儿到水秀山明的槟城去参观。蒙戴云峰兄的盛意，替我在升旗山顶，及丹戎武雅的海滨借到友人的宽敞清幽的别墅，一星期的眺水观山的生活，使我顿忘多年来整天绞脑汁的辛苦。

　　那次旅行，全程不过13天，内子的体重增加了5磅，亮儿结交了不少朋友。回家后，我问内子说："旅行之乐乐如何？"她频频点头，而且自告奋勇地要写一篇散文，记叙旅行的乐趣。时间一天一天过去，一直过了18个月，她拟作的游记还没有交卷。我知道家务的繁重，早已使一般受过相当教育的主妇失去写作的情绪。因此，我也不再催促她，只好自己动笔来写。

　　自这篇文字发表后，我写作的兴趣又浓厚起来，于是一篇又一篇，继续不断地往下写。其中有一次因为饮食不慎，肚子剧痛，两天没有吃东西，到了第三天健康稍微恢复的时候，我又抖擞精神，熬了一夜，把要写的文字写出来。积少成多，从去年圣诞节那一天起，到了今年五月间止，本书已经写成。

自五四运动以来，青年问题才引起社会人士注意。青年问题，千言万语，归纳起来，不外读书问题、革命问题、恋爱问题、职业问题、修养问题。新加坡是英国的殖民地，在今年四月民选立法委员以前，一般明哲保身的人，连"政治"两字也讳莫如深，更不敢高谈什么革命的理论或实践了。现在各地多是男女合校，社交十分公开，而且在南大①没有开办以前，这儿华校的最高学府主要的是中学。中学生年纪这么轻，衣食由父兄供给，他们应该拼命地读书，所以恋爱问题、职业问题没有谈的必要。说来说去，还是读书问题和修养问题，才是他们的切身问题，虽然课外活动也应该兼顾。

关于读书的过程，我在《回首四十年》里曾略述个人的经历，同时，特辟一章《谈治学方法》，这儿用不着多说，所以本书主要是谈青年的修养。

科学社会主义的创始者告诉我们："不是人类的意识决定人们的存在，倒是社会的存在决定人们的意识。"因此，有志气的青年，必须选择环境，适应环境，甚至要充分利用环境。

---

① 南大：南洋理工大学。

年来我曾以三事鼓励青年：身体好，读书好，大家相亲相爱。后来我看报载国内的导师也鼓励青年注意三事：身体好，学习好，工作好。这种平易近情的目标，大家可说是不约而同。须知健康是一切幸福的源泉，同时也是我们最可靠的资本。有了健康，整天精神愉快；没有健康，简直如坐愁城。我希望每个有志气的青年，在锻炼雄伟的体魄上应该痛下功夫，这才能够负起社会所付给他的责任。

本来学习和工作是分不开的。从广义来看，学习和工作等于读书。活到老，读到老；读到老，读不完。你瞧，一个人拼命地读书，还读不了多少；假如坐此山，看彼山，一曝十寒，那他的成就一定大受限制。

中外的至圣大贤教人，须着重有本有源的学问，在没有做学问之前，须做真心诚意的功夫，所以本书对于"立志""计划""准备""勤力"等基本课题，都不惜浪费笔墨，反复说明。像画师必须先预备一尘不染的雪白纸张一样，有志学习的青年，必须志虑忠纯、心术善良。不然，认识错误，观念乖张，态度傲慢，一切学问适足以济奸，而热衷名利的人，不但对于国家、对于社会毫无贡献，说不定还会成为时代进化的绊脚石呢。

生在这时代的青年，须以维护世界和平为己任，因为目前核武器进步一日千里，除非世界和平，否则我们的子孙将做炮灰，而人类文化也将沦于危殆的地步。

因为我对于青年的期望很大,所以我知无不言,言无不尽。好在本书并非说教,而是笔谈,我只把青年所关心而又没有得到答案的问题,一一提出。除说明原则外,我尽量取譬引喻,一来希望他们容易了解,二来希望增进阅读的趣味。

至于本书各篇的题目,有的用成语,有的用诗句,我的目的并非掉书袋,而是我深切地觉得中国的许多成语和诗句是经过千锤百炼,百读不厌的。例如《论交友》这个题目,小学生可以做,中学生也可以做,我这儿却用楚辞《乐莫乐兮新相知》,这在文学的联想上,意义也许更深长些。又如《论反战》那个题目,大学教授可以做,报馆主笔也可以做,而俄国小说泰斗托尔斯泰竟以《战争与和平》这题目,写成四厚册,我这儿却用唐诗"一将功成万骨枯"的名句,写成一篇散文。可惜我读书不多,经验不够,不然,我真想仿效托尔斯泰的办法,把这个浅近的题目写成洋洋大观的巨著。

本书仅代表我个人对于青年的修养问题的意见,聊供课外参考。我知道青年是最坦白最率真的。假如我所说的有不对的地方,希望各地青年不吝指教。

1955年9月9日深夜连士升志于新加坡

目 录

1　一年之计在于春　　1
2　饱带干粮晴带伞　　4
3　为有源头活水来　　7
4　专精一艺可成名　　10
5　老大谁能更读书　　13
6　山雨欲来风满楼　　16
7　长江后浪推前浪　　20
8　是非只为多开口　　23
9　冤仇宜解不宜结　　27
10　一失足成千古恨　　30
11　花未全开月未圆　　34
12　功名不上懒人头　　37
13　江南望见江北好　　40
14　七分锣鼓三分唱　　43
15　月到中秋分外明　　47
16　吃药三年会行医　　51
17　旅行之乐乐如何　　54
18　乐莫乐兮新相知　　57

19	长得俏来才是俏	60
20	响遏行云横碧落	63
21	花木成蹊手自栽	66
22	万物静观皆自得	69
23	又得浮生半日闲	73
24	乡音无改鬓毛衰	76
25	一将功成万骨枯	79
26	安得广厦千万间	82
27	天生我材必有用	85
28	人到无求品自高	88

1　一年之计在于春

> 少有大志的人，不见得个个会成功，但是少无大志的人，我敢断定他会随波逐流，毫无主张，一事无成。

"一年之计在于春，一日之计在于晨，一生之计在于勤。"这说明凡事在草创的时期，须立定基础，然后才能够繁荣滋长，开花结籽，不然基础既不好，培植又失时，将来难免要失败。

当大地回春，万象更新的正月，一切都得作全盘的打算。只要计划定得合理，以后按部就班地实施，到了年终，来个总结算，看看今年的计划是否能够全部实现。假如不能实现，那么须检讨失败的原因在什么地方，并且找出补救的办法，作明年订计划的张本①。

就一天而论，早晨的时间实在太宝贵了。一个人经过晚上八小时的安眠后，精神全部恢复过来。这时候，空气特别清新，东升的太阳发出万丈的光芒，人们面对这个良好的自然环境，心情不消说十分愉快，这时候，你如果聚精会神地做两三个钟头功夫，它的效果比较白天在办公室忙碌了七八个钟头还大。俗语说得好："早起三日当一天。"其实清晨的饱满精神，无论做什么事情都很适宜。假如你善用清晨的时间，专心有恒地从事毕生的事业，那么前途一定十分光明。

谈到青年，这更是一个人的黄金时代。中国古代的史家，他们在写成名或成功的人的传记时，开头便说，某某人"少有大志"。的确，少有大志的人，不见得个个会成功，但是少无大志的人，我敢断定他会随波逐流，毫无主张，一事无成。所谓"大志"就是指抱负，用流行的俗语来说，即伟大的计划。

我常说，中学时代是一个人最重要的时代。因为小学时代，年纪太小，消化和吸收的能力很有限，到了大学后，老师仅站在指导的地位，基础较好的学生得益不少，基础太差的学生，老师向他讲解，简直是对牛弹琴[②]，笔记做得太慢，参考书看不明白，写报告简直难如登天。这种学生姑且能够混到一张文凭，但于人于己，两无是处。只有中学这阶段，消化和吸收的能力最强，老师人格的陶冶，基本功课的训练，学习兴趣和方法的养成，正是做一天有一天的成绩，做一学期有一学期的效果。我们只看风云人物中，有好几位先生仅受过中等教育，但他们在学术上、功业上的成就远胜许多得过什么学位的人。可见中学时代基础打得好的人，以后进可以攻，退可以守。

其实，做学问要有计划，盖屋子要有计划，治国平天下更应该有计划。越王勾践的十年生聚③，十年教训，可说有史以来最早给国计民生定计划的大政治家。从个人到社会，从一个国家到整个世界，凡百事业，有计划总比没有计划的盲目乱撞高明万倍。我们知道世间不如意事常八九，许多有意义的计划，不见得个个能够实行，说不定在没有实行之前早已流产；但我们确信，假如没有计划，那是绝对不行的。而平易近人的计划，比好大喜功④的计划更易见效。

老实说，假如我明白你的志愿或抱负，那么你未来的一切行动，不用开口，我也明白了大半。

1955年3月27日深夜

注释：

① 张本：为事态的发展预先所做的安排。

② 对牛弹琴：比喻对不懂道理的人讲道理，完全无用。

③ 十年生聚：生聚，繁殖人口，聚积物力。指军民同心同德，积聚力量，发愤图强。

④ 好大喜功：好，喜欢。一心想做大事、立大功。多形容浮夸、铺张的行为。

2　饱带干粮晴带伞

> 其实，差不多每个人都有机会发展他的雄图，不过大多数人的准备功夫做得太差，等到机会来时，他们一点也把握不住。在人生斗争的过程中，胜败可说是常事。最后的胜利，归于那些有充分准备的人。

　　在中国的农村社会里，中等以上的家庭，照例在大厅上悬挂联板字画，在各种各色的联板和字画中，《朱伯庐①治家格言》可以说是普遍地受人欢迎。朱伯庐教人："宜未雨而绸缪②，勿临渴而掘井。"不过我觉得这两句格言远不如"饱带干粮晴带伞"那一句更通俗，更富有积极的精神。

　　聪明人和普通人不同的地方，就是前者把事情看得远一点，所以棋先一着，占尽便宜。普通人走一步，算一步，凡事毫无准备，一遇三长两短，便慌慌张张，怨天尤人。其实，世界上任何事情都受"因果律"的支配的,专家虽不会比普通人更聪明,但他特别注意"因果律",知道来龙去脉,所以他才有先见之明。只因他能够"先见"或"预知",事前稍加准备,临事沉着应付,精神集中,方寸不乱,谈笑间把大事化为小事,小事化为无事。

一个人有没有学问,全看他过去所受训练的程度、平时用功的方法、搜集资料的功夫、结交良师益友的多寡而定。对于某一个问题,假如平时下过真功夫,那么下笔为文的时候,才会深入。假如他平时没有做过准备的功夫,胸无点墨,虽搜索枯肠,恐怕也要交白卷。

其实,差不多每个人都有机会发展他的雄图,不过大多数人的准备功夫做得太差,等到机会来时,他们一点也把握不住。真正懂得运筹帷幄③的人会制造机会,普通人多少会利用机会,只有平时漫不经心,毫无准备的人,才眼巴巴地让一次一次好机会跑掉了。

在人生斗争的过程中,胜败可说是常事。最后的胜利,归于那些有充分准备的人。因为事业的成功不是走直线的,中间须经过许多迂回曲折,起伏升沉的阶段。第一道防线破了,还有第二道;第二道防线坏了,还有第三道。屡败屡战,再接再厉,熬过难关,便是好汉。假如平时没有好好地准备,一遇危机,马上便要缴械了。

《伊索寓言》载野猪和狐狸的故事。一只野猪站在树底下,对着树干磨砺它的獠牙。一只狐狸走过，问它在没有危险、没有遇到猎人或猎狗来恐吓的时候，为什么这样的磨砺它的牙齿。它回答道："我曾经仔细想过才这样做的，因为危险来临的时候，我应该运用我的獠牙，来不及去磨砺了。"这种居安思危的精神，是生存竞争应有的精神。

认真唱京戏的人，不管当天是否要出场，每日清晨总要起来吊嗓子。真正玩拳术的人，不管当天是否要比赛，每日总有铁定的时间从事练习。所谓"拳不离手，曲不离口"，就是这意思。不然，平时毫无准备，到了比赛的前夜，才连忙开夜车，弄到头昏脑涨，六神无主，不用交手，便决定胜负了。

准备功夫并不是白费的，它给我们节省了不少的时间和精力。为强调准备功夫的重要性，我们须记得"饱带干粮晴带伞"。

1955年1月13日清晨

注释：

① 朱伯庐：清初理学家（1617—1688）。他的《治家格言》，世称《朱子家训》，流传很广。

② 未雨绸（chóu）缪（móu）：趁着天没下雨，先修缮房屋门窗，比喻事先做好准备。

③ 运筹（chóu）帷（wéi）幄（wò）：运，运用；筹，筹划、制订计划；帷幄，古代军中的帐幕。在帐幕中策划军机要事。泛指策划、指挥。

3　为有源头活水来

> 一个人如要在学问上出人头地，必须在年轻的时候，把学问的基础打得很扎实，以后才能够开花结籽。

半亩方塘一鉴开，
天光云影共徘徊。
问渠那得清如许？
为有源头活水来。①

——[宋]朱熹《观书有感》

朱熹这首诗，不是普通诗人的诗，而是学道有得的诗。世间唯有本有源的东西，才能够取之不尽，用之不竭。不然，根底太浅，源流太短，一下子就用得精光，上气接不着下气，那狼狈的样子，实在够受了。

青年们须知文章要写得好，全在于平时"读书多，积理富"，尤其时常做笔记，把心得的见解、有用的材料一一记载下来；再进一步，把自己所读的书籍加上底线和眉批②，并且自编一索引。这样一来，到了需要作文的时候，只需把有关的东西，一加排比，删其芜杂，存其菁华，材料绝对不成问题。材料既然不成问题，那么这篇文章便算是"言之有物"了。假如平常对于名家著作的阅读十分留心，注意人家怎样谋篇、布局、造句、用字，怎样使文章有风趣、有神韵，几经锻炼揣摩，学习修改，那么在行文上就不至于"言之无文"了。内容充实，条理整齐，见解正确，文字畅达，这刚好达到"为有源头活水来"的境界。到那时，文思源源而来，滔滔不绝，无论写长篇，作短文，都觉得绰有余裕的乐趣，哪里还要搜索枯肠？

就近代英国文学而论，没有一个人的成就会赶得上萧伯纳③。萧伯纳自幼精通音乐，精研先辈绥夫特④的作品，光是这种本领，已够他成为很有资格的艺术批评家和幽默家。及长，他专攻当时风靡全欧的易卜生⑤的戏剧，同时，他著了一部《易卜生主义精华》(The Quintessence of Ibsenism)。渊源有自，取精用宏，所以他动笔写问题戏剧的时候，笔锋滔滔不绝，佳作层出不穷。

一个人如要在学问上出人头地，必须在年轻的时候，把学问的基础打得很扎实，以后才能够开花结籽。换句话说，在中学这阶段里，你没有把运用中文和英文的能力培养成功，以后任你读大学、研究院，也是徒然。你也许在其他部门的学问上得到一些知识，但你的吸收和表现的能力将大受限制。同样地，在中学这阶段，数学的基础打得不稳，以后你如果想专攻数、理、化等课程，恐怕也是吃力不讨好。至于音乐，现在一般有教养的家庭，多数让五六岁大的幼童开始学习，到了二十岁左右，早已成为音乐专家了。假如儿童的时期让它虚度过去，到了社会谋生的时候，对外有人事的纠纷，对内有生活的负担，整天纷纷扰扰，精神没有片刻宁静，哪里有闲工夫让你从头打好基础？

年轻的朋友们，假如你们懂得源头活水的可贵，那么你们应趁早从事有本有源的学问，不做道听途说、人云亦云的事情。只有这样，你们才能够有特立独行的思想、明辨是非的判断力，而这些东西是每个思想家、学者、文人应具备的首要条件。

1955 年 5 月 1 日劳动节

注释：

① 诗解：半亩大的池塘像明镜一样，映照着来回闪动的天光云影。要问这池塘怎么这样清澈？原来有活水不断从源头流来啊。

② 眉批：在书眉或文稿上方空白处所写的批注。

③ 萧伯纳：G. Bernard Shaw(1856—1950)，英国著名的剧作家和艺术批评家。

④ 绥夫特：Jonathan Swift(1667—1745)，英国作家，著作包括《大人国与小人国游记》(*Gulliver's Travels*)。

⑤ 易卜生：H. J. Ibsen(1828—1906)，挪威著名的剧作家，著作包括《玩偶之家》(*A Doll's House*)。

4　专精一艺可成名

> 在这个时代，常识的基础要广大，专门学问的造诣要精深。真正的学人或艺人，必须按自己的个性和环境，选择一两门学科，毕生专心研究。

俗语说得好："百艺通，没米舂。"这是说，一个人对于每种技能都粗通一点，但没有一样达到精通的地步。结果，穷途潦倒，一事无成，连日常生活也发生问题。

本来人类的天赋不同，有的是向单方面发展的，有的是向多方面发展的。在理论上，向单方面发展的人可以成功，向多方面发展的人不见得不会成功。不过一个人的时间和精力很有限，精于这方面的人，难免在另一方面荒疏，所谓顾此失彼，就是这意思。

在百科全书或名人小传里，一开头我们便见到这字样，某某人，什么家。如吉朋（Edward Gibbon），史学家；狄更斯

(Charles Dickens),小说家；凯恩斯(John Maynard Keynes),经济学家……一个学者或艺人,很可能兼具几种特长,但历史上仅记载他的最高峰的成就,其余的多略而不提。事实上,一个人如在一门学术上或艺术上,甚至功业上有特殊的造诣,已经可以闻名于世,假如样样都求精通,结果难免庸庸碌碌,一窍不通。久而久之,便被历史所淘汰。

谈到中国的书法,谁也不会忘记那位承先启后的书圣王羲之。王羲之以写字为专业。他先吸收汉碑魏碑的精华,然后神而明之,形成他独特的作风,而"铁画银钩"四字,最能道出他独特的作风。但是,我们须记住,他并非什么"生而知"的天人,而是普通"困而知"的常人。只因他把握住作书的方法(永字八法),又加上临池①的工夫,所以当他写字的时候,全力贯注,得心应手,有如神授。虽然在中国文学史上,他以书牍②出名,但他最大的成就却在于书法,而他的书法是以毕生的心血换来的。

去年我曾看过毫芒③雕刻家黄老奋的刻字,那笔画的纤细、笔迹的分明、行列的整齐,真是一丝不苟。我看他雕刻的时候,聚精会神,屏息吞声,手儿蠕蠕而动。刻完之后,肉眼看不分明,须用放大镜来观察,才充分领略他的功夫的精到。这虽小技,但他至少要花上一二十年功夫,才可问世。

事实告诉我们,一个人肯不断地专攻一门学术或艺术,成功仅是时间问题。

现在科学日益进步，分工越来越细密，一个人必须有一技之长，才可以安身立命④。除极少数特殊的人不受限制外，普通高中毕业生，须再受五至七年的专门训练，然后才可以当医生、律师、会计师、工程师、音乐师，至于纯粹的文学、史学、哲学及自然科学，学习的时间更是漫无限制。得到学位的人，至多可说是摸到门径，至于登堂入室的发明发现等工作，还须以后不断地努力。

在这个时代，常识的基础要广大，专门学问的造诣要精深。真正的学人或艺人，必须按自己的个性和环境，选择一两门学科，毕生专心研究。一面要虚心请教，一面要不断用功。现在应该是"日新，日日新，又日新"。三天不读书，茅塞顿生。在这种情形下，你不能不读书。事实上，只要你肯用心研究，迟早总有豁然贯通的一天。

1955年4月3日深夜

注释：

① 临池：相传汉代书法家张芝在水池旁边练习写字，经常用池水洗砚台，使一池的水都变黑了。

② 书牍（dú）：书信。

③ 毫芒：即毛的尖梢。毫芒雕刻就是精细微雕。

④ 安身立命：安身，在某处安下身来；立命，精神有所寄托。指生活有着落，精神有寄托。

5　老大谁能更读书①

> 一个中年或老年人，他的精力不如青年那么旺盛，而他的家庭负担繁重，人事关系的纠纷，简直弄到他没有一刻宁静的心情。在心烦意懒的状态下，连报也懒得看，更不用说要读什么书了。

青年的时代，真是一个人的黄金时代。在青年时代，读书固然容易进步，玩乐也是够痛快。简单说一句，青年时代，无论做什么行业，都不难达到出色当行的地步。

固然我们同意"大器晚成"的说法，不过这儿所谓"晚成"，是指准备的时间较长，成名的时间较晚，并不说是青年时期毫无准备，整天束书高阁②，好像守株待兔的笨汉那样，期待"晚成"。我承认书本知识仅算是学问的一部分，但它无疑的是最重要的部分。因为书本记载着古今中外的名人的经验，读者可以把他们的经验做基础，或者以他们的经验来做参考，然后再加上自己的经验。只有这样，他才有大成就。不然闭着眼睛，漠视前人或时贤的经验，什么事情都要自己来干一遍，恐怕人类文化永远不会进步。

本来学问没有止境的，活到老，学到老；学到老，学不完。不过同样的学习，青年好过中年，中年胜似老年。古人早有"少壮不努力，老大徒伤悲"的感慨。

青年精力的充沛，这一点谁也知道。最重要的是他不必忧虑家务，可以全力以赴地读书。另一方面，一般中年人也许因为先天不足，后天亏损，到了四十岁左右，已经呈现"而视茫茫，而发苍苍，而齿牙动摇[3]"的未老先衰的状态。青年一天到晚做不累的事，一般中年人仅做三四个钟头，已经连气也喘不过来。精力的衰退，使他对于人生的前途，从灿烂的金黄色，改为渺茫的灰暗色。

精力的衰退，已经是个很大的负担，最麻烦的就是要谋生。许多人都是所学非所用，所用非所学，要找到适当的工作来发挥特出的才具，颇不容易。就算你能够找到称心的工作，你还要应付许多意想不到的人事问题。

你瞧，一个中年或老年人，他的精力不如青年那么旺盛，而他的家庭负担繁重，人事关系的纠纷，简直弄到他没有一刻宁静的心情。在心烦意懒的状态下，连报也懒得看，更不用说要读什么书了。

在旧时代里，中国最有学问的人算是高僧。高僧的生活问题解决，加以他们"赤条条来去无牵挂"，人事的纠纷也减少了许多。他们响应晨钟的号召，天未黎明即起来念经。几部重要的佛典，费了几十年的工夫翻来覆去的朗诵、默念、潜思，只要中等的天资，也可以念出一些道理来。这证明"老大"还能够读书，还能够做学问。不过这种机会并不多，一般人一经离开学校，学问的前途便大受限制。除非他们老早养成读书的习惯、治学的能力，使他们懂得忙里偷闲地珍惜一分一秒的时间，并且懂得充分利用这一分一秒的时间，否则进步恐怕很困难。

"老大谁能更读书"，这并不是给中年人浇冷水，而是警告一般青年须趁精力充沛、生活无忧、心情宁静的时候打好基础，因为将来开花结籽的情形，全看青年所打下的基础的深浅而定。

1955 年 10 月 2 日于海景酒店

注释：

① 老大谁能更读书：取自唐代诗人王缙（王维的弟弟）的诗："身名不问十年馀，老大谁能更读书？林中独酌邻家酒，门外时闻长者车。"

② 束书高阁：束，捆扎；高阁，储藏器物的高架。把书捆扎起来放在高高的架子上，比喻弃之不用。

③ 出自韩愈《祭十二郎文》。

6　山雨欲来风满楼

> 我劝大家多读历史。除一国的通史外，干各行业的人，须明了该行的历史，这才能够洞悉过去，了解现在，把握将来。

懂得因果律的人，对于事情的前因后果的关系搞得很清楚。他知道一件事情并不是凭空发生的，一定有它之所以发生的原因；把握住它的原因，再推测它的演变和后果，真是"虽不中亦不远矣"。

中国古代的圣人对因果律十分考究。他们从哲学着手，到了哲学有相当把握后，便把它应用到人事上去，尤其军事、政治、经济，他们是更有心得。假如要用两句话来概括他们的理论，我觉得"见微知著①"和"因势利导②"这两句话是再恰当不过。前者注意因果律的研究，后者着重因果律的运用，研究既有心得，运用又十分得法，这才有左右逢源③、触类旁通④的乐趣。

在下雨之前，蚂蚁早已急忙地搬家。微小的蚂蚁既没有气象台做靠山，又没有各种仪器的配备，它们只凭经验，知道气压太低，地下潮湿，行动困难，于是赶紧搬家，从潮湿的低地，搬到干燥的高地。这样一来，他们才能够免得给水淹死。年轻的蚂蚁看到长辈这样做，实在很有道理，所以它们不知不觉也如法炮制，一遇气候要变动，它们便提前搬家。

读过经济学的人，谁都知道什么叫作"商业循环"（Business Cycle）。当商业繁盛的时期，凡百事业都欣欣向荣。人们表示积极乐观，银行也乐意多多放款。不幸在自由竞争的经济制度下，一切是漫无组织，毫无计划，有时某部门的工商业，因为投资过多，生产过剩，致供过于求，结果市场停滞，销路锐减，货物堆积如山。物主急急求售，便不择手段，把货物抛出。银行见形势不妙，于是实行紧缩，把有关的工厂和商行的放款抽回，工厂和商行因为存货没有销路，银行追款又急如星火，前无去路，后有追兵，在这双重势力夹攻下，周转便感不灵。结果，一部分工厂和商行只好关门大吉，有些负责人甚至自寻短见，一死了之。这样一来，市场混乱，百事萧条，不景气的程度达于极点。

当市场不景气的时候，有些幸运儿靠山雄厚，手段高明，得以逃过难关。他们吃了一次亏，学了一次乖，所谓大难不死，必有后福。他们比较从前更为小心，凡事稳扎稳打，发展市场，减少开支，开源节流，收支达到平衡。因为平时收支平衡，甚至有点余蓄，得以加强社会信用。到了机会来时，他们又可运用银行的资金，发展他们的企业。有时运用得法，不到一年半载工夫，利市十倍，一般商场又呈现欣欣向荣的状态。

总之，聪明人和平常人不同的地方，就是前者"见微知著"，凡事能够"前知"；普通人多是事后聪明，等到雨过天晴之后，这才恍然大悟刚才是遇着一场狂风暴雨。为补救这种缺陷，我劝大家多读历史。除一国的通史外，干各行业的人，须明了该行的历史，这才能够洞悉过去，了解现在，把握将来。因为我们现在的穷通利达是基于过去所种的因，而现在的勤惰智愚将结成将来的果。种瓜得瓜，种豆得豆，因果的关系，说来就是这么简单。

"山雨欲来风满楼"，这说明当前的一切迹象，可以告诉你今后的趋势。假如一个人不读历史，不观察当前的一切迹象，只知逆天背时，一意孤行，那么他的前途恐怕连最微小的蚂蚁也不如了。

1955年4月24日

注释：

① 见微知著：微，微小、细小；著，明显。看到事物的一点细小迹象，就能知道它的发展趋向。

② 因势利导：因，随顺，依着；势，趋势；利导，引导。顺着事物发展的趋势，很好地加以引导。

③ 左右逢源：逢，遇到；源，水源。处处可以遇到水源。原指学问很深，可以取之不竭，用之不尽。后比喻为人处事得心应手，非常顺利。

④ 触类旁通：触类，遇到某一类事物；旁，其他、别的；通，懂得。接触或掌握某一类事物的规律，就能推知相关方面的知识或规律。

7　长江后浪推前浪

> 学问是没有止境的,"自满"两字,在治学的过程中绝对用不着。相反的,学然后知不足,只因自己觉得不足,这才能够发愤图强地继续潜修。

"长江后浪推前浪,一代新人换旧人。"

无情的岁月,天天在暗中消逝。不管你进步或不进步,时间仍像滚滚长江东逝水一样,不舍昼夜地往前流。一个人到了 45 岁,还是一事无成,而后生小子却以充沛的精力,毫无家累地往前跑,不用几年工夫,你不想被淘汰,也要受淘汰了。

要避免时间的淘汰,必须不要自满。原来时间是继续不断地前进的。昨天轰动一时的新闻,今天已算是旧闻;再过两天,已经是明日黄花了。商汤究竟是个出色的元首,他的座右铭就是:"苟日新,日日新,又日新。"[①]的确,在这科学的进步一日千里的时代，一个人如自我陶醉、故步自封②，这等于宣告自杀。因为学问是没有止境的，"自满"两字，在治学的过程中绝对用不着。相反的，学然后知不足，只因自己觉得不足，这才能够发愤图强地继续潜修；博闻强记，身体力行，积累了相当时间，自有水到渠成的一天。

人类最大的毛病，在于不自知。虽然谁都承认自满是不对的，但是他个人是否已经陷于自满的状态，自己并不完全知道，同时，也没有一个人肯对他说明。一来年纪天天增加，老气横秋，人们对他采取"敬而远之"的态度；二来他在社会上也许已有些"地位"，紧握一些实权，老于世故的部属，凡事唯唯诺诺，谁肯对他说真话？

在人生的旅途中，所有旅客好像长途比赛的车辆。在出发点，每辆车表面上似乎是势均力敌；可是到了中途，有的机件发生故障，有的因驾驶者控制失灵，在路上翻筋斗。在这种场合下，参加比赛的其他车辆绝不会停下来，等你修理竣事后，才跟你携手并进。相反的，你的车辆出了事，是你个人的不幸或过失，人家不会原谅你。因为比赛场中根本没有什么客气和礼让，所以你的不幸或过失，只有你个人自作自受，人家不会替你受罪，或给你同情。其实，失败就是失败，本着"败军之将，不足以言勇"的古训，你还有什么话可说？

孔夫子这位先生到底有先见之明，他说："后生可畏，焉知来者之不如也？四十、五十而无闻焉，斯亦不足畏也已。"③的确，在科学研究的过程中，后来居上。"后生"所吸收的新学识、新经验，恐怕不是三四十年前的老学生所能想象得到。假如一般中年人以为自己薄有虚名，不想继续学习，那么他的前途就算完了。俗语说"盖棺论定"。我觉得不长进，没出息的人，可说是"没有盖棺而论已定"。

为避免受时间的淘汰，一个人只有不断学习，到处求师。到了学问天天进步的时候，后生小子将崇拜之不暇，哪里还会轻视你呢？相反的，自己不长进，只有后退，中间并没有停足的地步。你瞧，当后浪推前浪的时候，还有什么客气的呢？

注释：

① 苟日新，日日新，又日新：出自《礼记·大学》。意思是：如果能够每天除旧更新，就应保持天天除旧更新，不间断地更新又更新。

② 故步自封：出自《汉书·叙传》。指守着老一套，不求进步。也作固步自封。

③ 意思是：年轻人是值得敬畏的，怎么就知道后一代不如前一代呢？如果到了四五十岁时还默默无闻，那他就没有什么可以敬畏的了。

8　是非只为多开口

> 在谈话中，尽可能多讨论一些正经问题，少品评人物的是非得失。

"病从口入，祸从口出。"因为贪吃和爱说话是人类的通病，所以生理上的不健康，及人事上的纠纷，便层出不穷。

古代圣人早知言语容易出岔子，所以他们一再诫人勿多言。老子说："知者不言，言者不知。"[①]这话很有道理。聪明人知道事实胜于雄辩，凡事只需拿出具体的功绩作证明，用不着啰啰唆唆地多费唇舌。相反的，假如你拿不出具体的功绩给人家看，一味自吹自擂，这当然不是聪明人的行径。孔子对于语言更加小心。他反对"巧言令色"[②]，他赞成"刚毅木讷"[③]。他否定"御人以口给"[④]，他主张"敏于事而慎于言"[⑤]。事实上，一等聪明人是多做事，少说话；普通人是做多少，说多少；只有下流人一味"车大炮"[⑥]，言不顾行，行不顾言，说话只求快意于一时，一点也不负责任。幸亏人们不愿意听他的话，结果，自欺欺人，受损失的还是自己的信用和名誉。

人类生下来有一双耳朵，一张嘴巴。这分明教人多听人家的高论，少发自己的意见。事实上，刚好相反。三五个朋友聚在一起谈天的时候，大家都侃侃而谈。在任何会议里，各代表们更以争着发言为无比的光荣。谁都希望别人"请你听我讲"，可是自己却爱讲不爱听，世间矛盾的事情没有比这更厉害。

一个人如有得意的事情，至多是暗中欢喜，千万不可形于颜色，更不该到处向人夸耀。比较有社会经验的人，当人家向他"恭贺"的时候，他只好微笑地推说这是由于"幸运"，绝不宜大模大样地接受人家的赞赏。人家赞赏还不应该接受，自己妄自夸大更不必说了。尤其在失意人的面前，滔滔不绝地叙述自己的得意的事情，使听者相形见绌⑦，觉得十分难堪。说话的人不识相到这地步，如遇什么不愉快的事情，真是活该！

一般说来，在谈话的过程中，往往犯着两个大毛病：一面喜欢指责人家的短处，一面爱夸张自己的长处。本来指头有长有短，可是人们在背后评论别人的时候，只记得别人的短处，因而加油加醋，大事渲染，把别人拿来当作谈笑的资料。开别人的玩笑的人固然兴高采烈，不过这种话一传到对方的耳朵里，难免会造成冤家。因为"自卫"是人类的本能，每个人都懂得掩蔽自己的短处，免得被人知道。现在一个人的短处不幸被别人发现，而且给别人当作茶余饭后的谈话资料，所以他的愤慨的情绪，不问可知。

在朋友聚会中，最好让每个人都有说话的机会。万一有些新客掺杂在中间，主人应该想法逗他说话，免得"一人向隅⑧，满座为之不欢"。在谈话中，尽可能多讨论一些正经问题，少品评人物的是非得失。就算要提到健在的人，尽可能本着"隐恶扬善"的原则，多颂扬人家的特长，少指责人家的缺点。以鼓励代替批评，以同情代替斗争，这更能维系朋友的感情。

我说这些话，并不是要人家做个毫无主意的"好好先生"。我是说，在可能的范围内，不要扯破面皮，因为说人好话没有什么，说人坏话很可能给人以极大的伤害。"言语伤人吃不消"，这事情我们不能不留心。

1955 年 2 月 19 日清晨

注释：

① 知者不言，言者不知：有智慧的人不会胡乱说话，胡乱说话的不是智者。

② 巧言令色：巧言，花言巧语；令色，讨好的表情。形容花言巧语，虚伪讨好。

③ 刚毅木讷（nè）：刚，刚强；毅，坚毅；木，质朴；讷，言辞谨慎。孔子说有这四种品德的人就接近仁德了。

④御(yù)人以口给(jǐ)：御，抵挡，这里指辩驳；口给，话说得多而快。意思是靠一张利嘴与人往来。

⑤敏于事而慎于言：做事情要勤劳敏捷，而说话则要谨慎小心。

⑥车大炮：指吹牛、吹嘘、浮夸的意思。

⑦相形见绌(chù)：相形，互相比较；见，显现；绌，不足。相比之下，一方显出不足。

⑧向隅：面向墙角，比喻非常孤立或得不到机会而失望。

9　冤仇宜解不宜结

> 宽恕这个美德，中外的哲人都一样地推崇它。与其把自己的气量放得那么小，不如恢宏自己的风度，宽恕别人。

一般说来，冤仇往往是这样结成的：不是争名，便是争利；不是争权，便是争色。名、利、权、色这四宗事情是造成冤仇的主要原因。在考试场中，有的鳌头独占，有的却名落孙山。两个程度相差较远的人倒没有什么，最坏的就是两人势均力敌。在成败的竞争最尖锐化的环境下，失败者难免要用阴谋诡计来中伤胜利者。到了这阴谋诡计发生破坏力的时候，与被损害的那一方，就要结成冤仇。目还目，牙还牙，冤仇相报，永无停止。

本来争名于朝，争利于市。在文坛或政海里，所争的是名次；在商场里，最重要的是财源广进。可是你想生财，人家也想进宝；财源有限，利欲无穷。在淡风吹遍市场、入不敷出的时候，他们可焦急了。于是假冒商标，偷天换日，行贿走私等把戏，层出不穷。假如这些阴谋诡计失败还算简单；万一成功，那么与受损害的一方，当然要结成冤仇了。

普通人只懂得求利，比较高明的人便想求名；再进一步，他们就要争取支配权。这野心是恺撒将军①雄长全欧的原因，也是他最后之所以遭人暗算，死于乱刀下的原因。至于《红楼梦》的凤姐，她在大观园里，并没有好好地享受人生的清福，一天就争着领导这个，看管那个，钩心斗角，为的是争取支配权。大权在手的人固然威风凛凛；无权无势的人，难免要想法生衅，中外古今关于这种掌故实在太多了，用不着多举。

在旧时代，婚姻多由父母做主，相对来说，较少人为争取恋爱的对象而闹到难解难分的地步，倒是风月场中，为着争风吃醋，搞到头破血流的较多。

由于争取名、利、权、色而结下巨恨深仇，这已经铸成大错；再进一步，就是采取各种手段来报仇。其实，所谓报仇，说穿了也很无谓。普通有权有势的人的报复方法，就是连芝麻大的事情，也请律师打官司，希望对方道歉，或赔偿"名誉"损失。有冤必报，有仇必复，这未免太不懂得幽默。

孔子说："成事不说，遂事不谏，既往不咎。"②宽恕这个美德，中外的哲人都一样地推崇它。与其把自己的气量放得那么小，不如恢宏自己的风度，宽恕别人。我们须注意，人家如对你不起，是出于有意，或起于无心？有心作恶又当别论，无心的过失是值得我们原谅的。因为人类是感情的动物，他看你不追究他的过失，他当然会感激涕零，说不定会改过自新，永远做个好人呢。

至于有意作恶的家伙，你与其费了吃奶的力量跟他争一日之长短，不如发动社会的力量来制裁他。反正"多行不义，必自毙"。因为小人的行径虽能侥幸得志于一时，但结果一定要遭清算，这事情我们是绝对相信的。

个人固然不应结冤仇，国家也不应该结冤仇。有些国家是到处无故寻仇觅恨，同时，还尽量发展武器，以便达到他们的目标。不知道从远处看来，这办法还是多余，因为战争胜负未卜，打输了固然有损失，赢了也要付出代价。

的确，冤仇宜解不宜结。这不但避免许多无谓的争执，而且是达到世界和平的大道。我们为什么不遵循正道，而自寻烦恼呢？

1955 年 3 月 6 日清晨

注释：

① 恺撒将军：Gaius Julius Caesar（前 102—前 44），古罗马政治家、军事家。

② 成事不说，遂事不谏，既往不咎：已做过的事不再解释，已完成的事不再劝说，过去的错误不再责备。

10　一失足成千古恨

> 我们既然知道胆小、心粗、气浮、志弱是万恶的原因，所以我们应该在提高涵养上下功夫，一面要胆大心细，一面要沉得住气，加强意志。

成功和失败，并不是一板之隔，有时二者的距离比较一张棉纸还薄。本来大奸似忠，大智若愚。奸和忠，愚和智，表面上好像绝对相反，事实上，奸和忠，愚和智，相差不过那么一点。所谓"差之毫厘，失之千里"，可以说是一语道破。

当一个人没有着手做事之前，他一定有"动机"或"念头"。动机纯正，念头善良，结果当然会利人利己；相反的，动机谬误①，念头恶劣，结果当然会干出那损人不利己的勾当。所谓种瓜得瓜，种豆得豆，这完全是因果律的运用，人力没法子挽回的。

一般说来，一个人的失败，环境算一半，个性也算一半。

虽然有的人把所有的原因推给环境，或者把一切责任加在个人身上，但这仅算是一偏之论，不足为训的。

一个人在创办任何事业的时候，必须具备胆识，所谓胆识是包括胆量和见识。因为初创办的事业，成功是未知数，没胆量的人既怕人讥笑，又怕会失败，结果连尝试也不敢，所以是注定的失败。

小胆粗心是失败的主因，要知道沉不住气也是自取灭亡之道。沉不住气的人会流于轻浮，在不应该说话的时间、地点和对象，他偏要发表意见。《三国演义》第七十二回载杨修之死，说他把曹操所提出的行军口号"鸡肋鸡肋"的谜底揭开，擅自收拾行装，准备归计；又把曹操所题的门内添个"活"字，解为丞相嫌园门太阔，代为再筑墙围，改造停当；又把曹操所写的"一合酥"解为"一人一口酥"，没得物主的同意，擅自分食；又把曹操假装梦中好杀人的诡计全盘揭破，说"丞相非在梦中，君乃在梦中耳"，诸如此类的事情，杨修虽一一猜对，但在某种场合下，这些话实在说不得。可惜杨修沉不住气，露才招忌，结果在"惑乱军心"的罪名下，身首异处。这儿可见沉不住气而又爱出风头的人，说小一点，会招侮辱；说大一点，会致杀身之祸。

我还要指出，意志懦弱，是一切罪恶、一切堕落行为的原动力。我有一位做小学校长的朋友，在偶然的机会到赌场去逛一逛。起初他连看也不敢看，后来由于好奇心的冲动，站在赌桌旁边参观,人家用现金换筹码来赌博,他仅在心里猜测,不幸每次猜测,都给他中的。在一本万利的金钱诱惑下,他的理智控制不住感情,所以他也想尝试赌的滋味。起初他仍站在旁边,在人家的赌注上加股,到了身上的现钞赌输一半的时候,他的心血来潮,这下子他顾不了什么师道的尊严,大模大样地坐下来,卷起双袖,拼命也赌。先把现金赌个精光,然后把手表和结婚戒指也脱下来做赌本,最后,欠了一身赌债,这才拖着疲倦的身躯回到宿舍。第二天消息传到董事部,董事部开个紧急会议,把这位没有资格为人师表的校长开除了。他受了这样突然而来的严重打击后,弄到六神无主,不久之后,便告失踪。当我听到他的噩耗②的时候,我不禁喊出"一失足成千古恨"!

成功和失败的确仅隔着一层薄纸。只要一念之差,成功和失败,判若两途。我们既然知道胆小、心粗、气浮、志弱是万恶的原因,所以我们应该在提高涵养上下功夫,一面要胆大心细,一面要沉得住气,加强意志。须知学好三年,学坏三天。十年辛苦经营的功业,可能在片刻之间毁坏净尽。

"一失足成千古恨。"到了失败之后,就是抢地呼天也是毫无办法了。

1955 年 3 月 20 日清晨

注释：

① 谬（miù）误（wù）：错误，差错。

② 噩（è）耗（hào）：指亲近或敬爱的人死亡的消息。

11　花未全开月未圆

> 全开的花一定全谢,全圆的月一定全缺。与其看全谢的花的东西飘零,全缺的月的到处黯淡,不如欣赏含苞未放的花的清香妩媚,将圆未圆的月的娟秀清华。前者是乐极生悲,后者才有无限的希望在前头。

假如东方文化可以用中国来做代表,那么我敢说,传统的中国文化精神,可由"花未全开月未圆"这句诗表现出来。

世俗的见解,总希望花常好、月常圆、人常寿,只有见识高人一等的哲人,才领略"花未全开月未圆"的滋味。这并非是普通的一句诗,它是中国哲人的人生观的总关键。

哲人并不是不欢喜花全开月全圆的。但是全开的花一定全谢,全圆的月一定全缺。与其看全谢的花的东西飘零,全缺的月的到处黯淡,不如欣赏含苞未放的花的清香妩媚,将圆未圆的月的娟秀清华。前者是乐极生悲，后者才有无限的希望在前头。

中国人最讲究含蓄。在文学上，我们注重弦外之音，言外之意。在园林的设计上，我们喜欢"曲径通幽处，禅房花木深"。具备深幽的环境，才可以谈到含蓄，不然，开门见山，一览无遗，真是毫无味道。

中国人很少打官司的，因为打官司的结果，输了固然可惜，赢了结怨更深。孔子曾说，他打官司的本领，并不比任何人差劲，但他总希望不要打官司。其实，中国人不但不爱打官司，而且以"交绝不出恶声"①为无上的美德。不然，把对方全盘压倒，将来狭路相逢，还有什么面目见人？

凡事须适可而止，这是最稳健的办法。假如事事都要求彻底——其实是无底的——恐怕麻烦的事情反而增加。当我看到世人自鸣得意地要彻底干他一下的时候，我不禁要念"花未全开月未圆"这绝妙的诗句出来。

由于经常观潮、望月、看花，我对于盈虚消长的道理颇能领略。观潮最好在潮水要涨到七八成的时候，浩浩荡荡，奔腾澎湃，心里也跟着兴奋。到了满潮时分，浪花四溅地打到岸上来，谁也要退避，不然，全身将给水淋湿，像个落汤鸡，那实在太煞风景。

到了潮水下退的时候，沙滩边留下一些腐烂的动物尸体，臭气冲天，气味很难闻。因此，我到海滨观潮的方法，多数都等到潮水已生，但还未达到满潮的时候，因为随着潮水的逐步高涨，它会带来一阵阵的海风，使人的精神比较振作。

　　根据前人的经验，和我个人的观察，我深刻地觉得"世事让三分，天宽地阔"这句格言很有道理。和我相熟的朋友，都知道我不爱跟人斗争，因为斗争是白费精力的。姑定现在侥胜一时，占了一些便宜，到了将来倒吐的时候，那可受不了。

　　因为严守"花未全开月未圆"的信条，我对于宁静、淡泊、谦和的大人物都表示三分敬意。甘地、泰戈尔是这种人；萧伯纳、罗素也是这种人；而淡恬寡欲的陶渊明，更是我最心仪②的老师。

　　"譬如饮不醉，陶然有余欢。"这才是懂得充分地享受"花未全开月未圆"的乐趣的人应有的态度。

1959 年 7 月 12 日清晨

注释：
① 交绝不出恶声：君子即使同别人断绝了交往，也不说对方的坏话。
② 心仪：心中仰慕。

12 功名不上懒人头

> 天才没有凭据,努力却有迹可循。成名须要不断地努力;但不断地努力,不一定能够成名。你瞧,努力既然不能够确保成名,那么懒惰更不用说了。

首先我要声明,世俗所谓功名,如金榜题名,如高官厚禄,都不在我所讨论的范围之内。我所指的功名,主要的是关于文坛艺苑最高的成就。这种成就,虽然和环境有关,但十九须看真才实学。

富兰克林教人"努力能克服困难,懒惰会制造困难"(Diligence overcomes difficulties. Sloth makes them.)。这话一点也不错。老实说,真正努力的人,也许有大成,也许有小就,但不努力的人,绝对没有成就,这一点明若观火。良师益友,至多能指示我们新的方法,或纠正一些错误,但他们对于我们的成就并没有多大帮助。"梓匠轮舆能与人规矩,不能使人巧。"①孟子这两句话，是他从艰苦中得来的经验之谈。

时间是无情的。它是一去不回头的。中国的诗人高唱"时光不待人"，外国的成语也说"Time and tide wait for no man"。因为生命是时间的累积。生命有没有意义，只看你每天的时间过得有没有意义。假如每天的时间都虚度过去，那么你的一生可算白活了。时间好像流水或白驹，转眼之间，不知道已经跑过了十年八载。到了一旦发现自己的精力已经衰退，才长叹一声"总角②闻道，白首无成"，恐怕已经来不及了。

成大功、立大业的人，并不会比较普通人多活许多年，他们只是充分利用他们的时间罢了。苏东坡和达·芬奇，一个代表中国的多才多艺的大文豪，一个代表西洋的博学多能的艺术家。他们仅活得中寿。他们的环境虽佳，天资虽高，但是最主要的是他们俩各具惊人的努力。苏东坡到了深夜还独自朗诵《阿房宫赋》，达·芬奇的速写簿及笔记积了 40 年之久。这些都是他们的真正本钱，而他们在文学上艺术上的表现，仅算是这些雄厚的本钱的运用罢了。

努力的方法，不外专心与有恒。专心是指专心一意。英文把专心写为"concentration of mind"（聚精会神）或"single-mindedness"（一心一意），这是很有意思的。事实上，专家所干的固然是专心一意的工作，即使多才多艺的通人所干的也是专心一意的工作。"千山万壑③，必有主峰。"通人懂的东西虽多，但各种知识和工具，都是用来达到他的最高的目标。明白这一点,我们才懂得专心一意的益处。

但是,专心还不够,我们还需要有恒。一般来说,有恒的功夫最难。许多人可以在心血来潮的时候,拼命干了几天。过了这阶段,他马上呈露心灰意懒的状态,连干什么也不起劲了,甚至把原定的计划完全放弃,一去不回头了。在这种情形下,他难免要见异思迁,从前的一切努力,等于完全浪费。

天才没有凭据,努力却有迹可循。成名须要不断地努力;但不断地努力,不一定能够成名。你瞧,努力既然不能够确保成名,那么懒惰更不用说了。

明白这道理,那么"功名不上懒人头"这句话,一看便可明白了。

1955年2月12日深夜

注释:

① 梓(zǐ)匠轮舆(yú)能与人规矩,不能使人巧:木匠或专做车子的匠人能够把制作的办法标准传给别人,却不能使人学到高明的技巧。

② 总角:古代未成年的人把头发扎成髻,幼年的意思。

③ 壑(hè):山沟或大水坑。

13　江南望见江北好

> 须知干一行，怨一行的态度是错误的。任何事业的成功，都是用心血精力换来的。只有你肯用心思，愿意卖力气，从工作本身找到真正的乐趣，那才是走上成功的坦途，那才是登堂入室的秘诀。

　　人类真是怪东西，做一行，怨一行。无论做什么事情，老是觉得自己太过吃亏，人家占尽便宜。

　　中外圣人早就看出人类的通病是明于观人，暗于观己，所以孟子警告人："明足以察秋毫之末，而不见舆薪。"[①]本来秋毫是最微细的东西，只因这是人家的过失，所以为着吹毛求疵起见，连秋毫那么小的东西也可以发觉出来。至于自己的过失，那是掩饰唯恐不及，虽眼前放着一车柴草也没法子看见。人己之间，竟有这么大的隔膜，你说奇怪不奇怪？

严格一点说，做一行，怨一行的人，多是没出息的人物。世间顶天立地的好汉，他们唯一的秘诀，就是严守岗位。先尽自己应尽的本分，绝不跟人家计较暂时的得失。他们既不取巧，又不投机，更不会发违心的言论。因为他们相信取巧、投机、乱发违心的言论，也许能够欺骗读者或观众于一时，但终究难免被人看破。只有一心一德地站在自己应守的岗位，久而久之，自己才能够争取读者和观众的信任。

在中外的历史上，我最喜欢那些以身殉道的人物，如屈原、文天祥、史可法、苏格拉底、耶稣、伽利略、甘地。他们何曾不爱生命，可是当生命和道义不可得兼的时候，他们宁杀身以成仁，舍身以取义。只因他们认为名誉、事业、文章，比较什么都可贵，所以你如想以万金之富去交换他们的名誉、事业、文章，他们绝对是敬谢不敏。你瞧，用生命和金钱来交换他们的事业，他们还不屑为，哪里会做一行，怨一行呢？

孔子说："朝闻道，夕死可矣！"[②]这种决绝的精神，就是孔子在饥寒交迫之下，仍不改志，坚决地实行"学而不厌，诲人不倦"[③]的精神，所以他能成为万世师表。同样的，耶稣教人："你应该在人家面前承认救主。"这句话对于献身社会事业的青年更有特别的意义。因为你既然以身献给事业，你绝不能稍微遇着困难，便临阵逃脱，或者自打嘴巴。

须知干一行，怨一行的态度是错误的。任何事业的成功，都是用心血精力换来的。只有你肯用心思，愿意卖力气，从工作从本身找到真正的乐趣，那才是走上成功的坦途，那才是登堂入室的秘诀。不然，坐此山，看彼山；干这行，想那行，整天把大好时光去计较人家的是非得失，不想脚踏实地干自己应干的事情，结果，心浮意懒，无精打采，恐怕连糊口也成问题，还谈什么成大功，立大业？

"江南望见江北好"，这纯粹是好吃懒做、投机取巧的人的想法。真正献身于事业的人，应该尽心尽意尽力地守着自己的岗位，只有这样，才能够加强自信心，同时，自信心坚强的人，才能够争取人家的信任！

1955 年 4 月 17 日于勿洛海滨

注释：

① 明足以察秋毫之末，而不见舆（yú）薪：秋毫，鸟兽在秋天新长的细毛，比喻微小的事物。意思是说眼力能看到一根毫毛的末梢，而看不到一车柴草。比喻只看到小处，看不到大处。

② 朝闻道，夕死可矣：一个人早晨明白了真理，即使当晚就死，那也可以说是并没有虚度一生。

③ 学而不厌，诲人不倦：做人要不断学习，不感到厌烦；教育学生要有耐心，不感到疲倦。

14　七分锣鼓三分唱

> 他深知唱独角戏,是万不得已的办法,只要有机会,他一定会请志同道合的人来帮忙。合作的人越多,高才捷足的人更能够充分发挥他的力量,以便达到登峰造极的境地。

成功的梦想是很美丽的,但由梦想到实现,中间须经过很大的距离。固然一个人的成功需要聪明和努力,不过周遭环境的影响也不容我们一笔抹杀。大诗人一辈子努力的结果,还是屈服于环境的力量,于是大声高唱:"到老始知非力取,三分人事七分天。"所谓"人事",指个人的聪明和努力;所谓"天",指环境的影响。用更通俗的话来说,"七分锣鼓三分唱"。这虽是人人知道的俗语,不过里边却有大道理在。

成功的歌剧需要前台和后台的密切合作。假如一出歌剧没有一支最优秀的交响乐队，假如台上的布景不弄到惟妙惟肖①，假如各位配角不会举一反三，随时给主角制造机会，那么最重要的一二主角绝对没法子充分发挥他们的高明的艺术。只因参加演出的人对于整出歌剧都有具体的认识，无论主角也罢，配角也罢，跑龙套②也罢，指挥也罢，鼓手也罢，管理道具的人员也罢，控制灯光的技师也罢……谁都愿意在这出名剧的演出上多尽自己的本分，所以事前的积极准备、演出时的布线行针、落幕后的细心检讨，大家须运用高度的智慧、热烈的心情来促进全剧演出的成功。简单说一句，假如没有那么多无名英雄一致卖力气，一二主角也毫无用处。

戏剧上的"七分锣鼓三分唱"，普通人都能够领略。其实，这种原则在其他部门何曾不能应用？就建筑而论，北京的故宫之所以驰誉全球，因为它的气魄雄奇伟大，形式美轮美奂，材料精巧雅致，真是一点一滴，一弯一曲，一门一户，一梁一栋，无一不合规矩和法度，又无一不显出新奇和巧妙。尤其值得注意的是，天安门前的广场和长安街、故宫后边的景山，以及左边的太庙（今北京市劳动人民文化宫）、右边的中央公园（今北京中山公园），每处固有它的特色，可是和故宫排列在一起，更可烘托它的美丽。再进一步，整个北京城的又高又厚的城墙、井井有条的街道、四四方方的庭院，以及遍地浓荫的树木，使城中央的故宫的金碧辉煌的琉璃瓦③，像鹤立鸡群一样，有突出的表现。

音乐和建筑都是"七分锣鼓三分唱"，要看背景，要看周遭的环境。同样的，要做研究工作的人也离不开几个学术中心。所谓学术中心，主要的是由几个条件配合：最高学府、设备完善的图书馆和实验室、出类拔萃的学者。这种学术中心，一个国家找不到三五处，有的国家仅有一处。真正研究学问的人，宁愿在学术中心挨饿，不愿意到文化落后地区去享受鱼翅燕窝。为什么呢？一个学者一离开学术中心，简直如鱼失水，精神上完全缴械。

一个人深明"七分锣鼓三分唱"的道理后，他再也不敢卖弄才华，闭着眼睛，乱"车大炮"了。他深知唱独角戏④，是万不得已的办法，只要有机会，他一定会请志同道合的人来帮忙。合作的人越多，高才捷足的人更能够充分发挥他的力量，以便达到登峰造极的境地。

现在是谈健全组织的时代。凡百事业，都注重集体创作。在这时代里，我提出"七分锣鼓三分唱"，不会毫无意义吧。

1955年1月9日清晨

注释：

① 惟妙惟肖：妙，巧妙；肖，相似。形容描写、刻画或模仿得非常巧

妙逼真。

②跑龙套：在戏剧中扮演随从或兵卒。

③琉璃瓦：表面用玻璃烧成的瓦，多呈绿色或金黄色，鲜艳发光，多用来修建宫殿或庙宇等。

④唱独角戏：独角戏，只有一个角色的戏。比喻一个人独自做某件事（通常需要多人做的）。

15 月到中秋分外明

> 人逢喜事精神爽,月到中秋分外明。人生几十年,写意的环境实在不可多得。当我们遇到较好的环境的时候,我们应该充分利用它来发挥我们的智慧和能力,这才有更大的成就。

一年虽有十二个月,但每个月中不见得都是明月团圆,有时遇着阴雨,有时遇着大雾,冬天既太冷,春夏之交又太潮湿,七除八抹,一年仅剩了一个中秋。

当旧历八月中旬,秋深气爽,云层很高,湿度较低,浓雾更消散得无影无踪。天上没有一片云彩,一轮皓月,独挂高空,月色的妩媚,月光的皎洁,月影的婆娑,无一不提高月儿的地位。

"月到中秋分外明"这句话很有深刻的意义,它证明时间和空间配合得适当,然后会发生特殊的影响。不然,在逆天背时的环境下，同一举动，会发生不同的结果。

俗语说："争名于朝，争利于市。"京师是人文荟萃①的地方，各种人才应有尽有。假如你自问在某部门的学术或艺术有特殊的成就，你就应该跑到京师去一显身手。那儿有万流景仰的大师，有眼光独到的批评家，一登龙门②身价十倍。退一步说，假如你肯虚心学习，京师有的是机会。只要你不自满、自足，你尽可向那些和你的专门学艺有关的前辈或同辈，质疑问难③；一经纠正，宛若画龙点睛，而你的心里也会觉得"实迷途其未远，觉今是而昨非"④的乐趣。从此加功，迟早也有大成就，这比较一个人独自暗中摸索，强胜万倍。

至于争利于市，这道理更容易明了。现代的大城市，都分成住宅区、文化区、工业区、商业区、政府机关区。就商业区而论，几十家银行必须集中，造成金融中心；几家百货商店必须互相毗连，借收彼呼此应之效。顾客从这家百货商店进去，从那家出来，进进出出，好像跑过连绵不断的走廊。再进一步，在中央市场里，鸡、鸭、鱼、肉、青菜、杂货、零食摊分据各层楼的每一角落，井井有条，一点也不混乱。从表面上看来，许多同行的商店排列在一起，生意的数量和利润似乎会减少；事实上，刚好相反。第一，同行的商店一集中，它们马上会造成一个中心区，顾客不买某种东西则已，要买某种东西，非到那儿去采购，心里老是不舒服。在贸易的总量上，那个已经造成中心区的市场，无形中比较那些孤零零的商店增加了好几倍。第二，因为同行的商店集中在一个地方，它们在集体采购方面，可以节省许多手续和运费，结果使成本减低。第三，现代商业受大规模生产的工业的影响，薄利多卖，是赚钱的不二法门。现代中央市场的买卖既然做得多，它们所得到的利润也很可观。因此经营现代企业的人，必须在各企业最繁盛的区域占了一席地，这才够资格。

"月到中秋分外明"，为的是中秋的明月在时间和空间上配合得特别好，让她显出她的真面目。明白这道理，我们才知道为什么一个人不要在家里泡一壶茶，形单影只地作牛饮，偏要跑到人声鼎沸的茶楼去跟朋友们谈天说地；为什么一个人不关了门拿一本书来阅读，偏要跑到万头攒动的大图书馆去做研究工作；为什么一个人不甘心在小球场里锻炼，偏要费了那么多金钱，前往全国运动会、世界运动会去观摩。因为在时间和空间配合得当的环境中，心情特别兴奋；而兴奋的心情，才容易给人以灵感，予人以原动力。须知肯干未必都能够达到预期的目的，不干简直是毫无希望。人逢喜事精神爽，月到中秋分外明。人生几十年，写意的环境实在不可多得。当我们遇到较好的环境的时候，我们应该充分利用它来发挥我们的智慧和能力，这才有更大的成就。

注释：

① 人文荟(huì)萃(cuì)：各种文化聚集在一地。

②登龙门：比喻得到有力者的援引而增长声誉。

③质疑问难：提出疑难问题来讨论。

④ 实迷途其未远，觉今是而昨非：取之东晋文学家陶渊明（365—427）的《归去来辞》，意思是说走入迷途确实还不太远，认识到如今做得正确而过去十分错误。

16　吃药三年会行医

> 向导多么可靠，工具多么精良，最后还需要我们自己去跑一趟，去学几次，才能够知道个中艰苦。同时，只有深明个中艰苦的人，才可以说是真才实学。

"久病成医"，或者"吃药三年会行医"，这说明实际的经验多么会增进人们的智慧。

本来百闻不如一见，百见不如一做。只有动手做过，才知道个中艰苦；同时，只有深明个中艰苦的人，才可以说是有真才实学。

人类从生食到熟食，从熟食到调和百味，预备美酒佳肴，中间有很大的距离。因为病从口入，吃得太多了，生病的机会也增加。到了生病的时候，家里人不得不替你医，可是那时没有医生，没有药铺，更没有医院，聪明的人曾尝过百草，看看哪种草适宜医治哪种病。无效的药物拉倒，有效的记录下来，第二次患同样的疾病的时候，可用同样的药物去医治。后来人口增加，社会人事复杂，于是实行分工合作，用不着每个人都要亲尝百草，只由少数专家负责医药。生病的人去看医生，医生给病人开个药方，到药铺去买药，自己不必再预备生草，这不消说是个大进步。

为什么说"久病成医"或者"吃药三年会行医"呢？因为平时生活过得相当舒服，时间过得很快。到了生病的时候，一切活动完全停止，整天对着药炉病榻，真是度日如年。在寂寞无聊的时候，恨不得病症早日离身，于是不识字的人，要向医生问长问短，日积月累，医药的常识无形中增加；识字的人更可以把医书拿来看，看不懂的请教医生，自己有心得的拿来应用。由于"试验与错误"（trial and error），久而久之，医理自明。虽然现代医学发达，非读六七年医学专科得不到医学文凭，但在从前医学幼稚的时候，一个人如看了三年医书，或者有两三年临床的经验，尽可挂牌行医了。

谈到医生，我不禁想起博士。因为博士的敲门砖比较普通人敲得更响，他们一置身社会，常可得到高官厚禄，这种不劳而获的过分优待，是使许多博士一辈子没出息的原因。因为他们一来就占较高的地位，颐指气使[①]，许多事情他们没有经手办过。由于经验缺乏，不知个中艰苦，所以乱发命令，随便责备人家，弄到人事缺乏协调，时常发生摩擦。甚至社会上有"二十是神童，五十是老而不死"的说法。这并非是博士学位的过失，而是得过这学位的人没有妥善运用的过失。

假如在学理上已经有相当修养的人，愿意在事业上从头做起，不取巧，不偷懒，前途实在是未可限量。因为书本的知识，仅算是前人的经验的结晶，假如没有亲自阅历过，绝对不知道其中艰苦，至多仅能算是人云亦云。

"在没有掌舵之前，一个人应该懂得划船。"（One should learn how to row before trying to take the rudder.）这句话对于有志成大功立大业的人，有特殊的意义。假如经验不够，一遇紧要关头，一定手忙脚乱，招架不来。相反的，只有充分的经验，能够履险如夷，才能够对天大的事情轻松应付。

我承认书本知识是人类的聪明睿智[2]之士几千年来累积的经验的结晶，它是我们的向导，可以节省我们暗中摸索的痛苦；它是我们精良的工具，可以节省我们不少的力气。但是，说句老实话，向导多么可靠，工具多么精良，最后还需要我们自己去跑一趟，去学几次，才能够知道个中艰苦。同时，只有深明个中艰苦的人，才可以说是真才实学。

1955 年 1 月 16 日清晨

注释：

① 颐 (yí) 指气使：不说话而用面部表情或口鼻出气发声来示意，指有权势的人随意支使人的傲慢神气。

② 睿 (ruì) 智：睿，看得深远。睿智，英明有远见。

17 旅行之乐乐如何

> "一山自比一山高",假如要知道山高不高,必须多旅行,这才有所比较。

在办公室里整天过着例行公务的生活的人,好像磨坊的驴马一样,门径摸得很纯熟,闭着眼睛也不轻易走错路。另一方面,因为生活缺少变化,刺激的东西太少,感觉比较迟钝,这不消说是个损失。事实上,作息调剂恰当,工作的效率肯定大大提高。

休息的方法,静不如动。因为长期过着办公室生活的人,处于人烟稠密的都市,体力活动的机会实在太少。因此周末最适宜到郊外去野餐、游泳、爬山、打球,至少也应该到附近公园的草地上伸伸腰,呼吸两口野花闲草的香气。当有长假时,当然以到国外游历为上策。

像绝代佳人的不易遇见一样,名山胜水也不算太多,新加坡仅是个小岛,这里不容易找到许多名胜,本是意中事。

但是，跑到国外，情形可就两样。同样的海景，地中海之滨的浪漫气氛和大西洋的严肃情调显然不同。同样一座山头，这些点缀着竹篱茅舍、小桥流水的东方景物，和那些常青树修剪得整整齐齐、把屋顶围墙涂得花花绿绿的西方景物又不同。俗语说得好："一山自比一山高。"假如要知道山高不高，必须多旅行，这才有所比较。

在交通发达的今天，旅行再方便不过。我常说：国民外交比较官方外交更见重要。官方外交多是言不由衷，国民外交是开诚布公①的。假如一个人要了解外国的人情风俗，他绝对不能单靠官方的统计，或者仅和政府大员晤谈。他应该和当地的中下级人士有所接触，这才能够找到真实的材料。而广泛的旅行，就是找寻真实材料的捷径。

真是"百闻不如一见"，许多事情本来不易明白，一看可明白了。假如看了还不明白，再加上"好问"的习惯，结果，就能够完全了解了。现代国家主持大计的人，都知道旅行的可贵，所以他们时常遣派专家到外国去参观与考察，在短时间内，各方面都有莫大的收获。

旅行不但能促进交情，增益见闻，而且给口腹以很大的实惠。我们固然知道故乡风味很不错，但是，各地方都有它的美酒佳肴，非亲历其境，尝不出它的味道来。远地的厨师可以请得来，远地的材料已经有点困难，远地的风景简直没有办法搬过来。只有在某种环境某种心情下，尝到了某种食物,才真正领略到它的好处。换了一个地方,再换了个心情,什么山珍海味都要走样了。

  旅行的乐处实在数不完。不过旅行需要相当多的金钱,相当强的脚力,更需要有谈得来的伴侣。人数多则四五人,少则一对。浩浩荡荡的大军人马的旅行团,实在太煞风景,跑在前面的三五个人还可以看到一点东西,站在后边的什么也看不着,听不清楚,尤其到工厂或其他机关参观的时候。假如没有适当伴侣,那么一个人单独旅行也不坏。反正现在交通十分便利,各大都市的旅行社林立,一个陌生人到了新地方,不怕没房子住,没有饭吃,就怕你没钱。

  从明年元旦起,我立志多读书,多写作,同时,须束紧腰带,节省开支。当旅费有相当把握,我准备向我服务的机关请假去旅行,我自信这笔钱是不会白花的。

1954 年圣诞节

注释:

  ① 开诚布公:开诚,敞开胸怀,表示诚意;布,宣布。形容发表或交换意见时态度诚恳,坦白无私。

18　乐莫乐兮新相知

> 朋友是可爱的。他是人生的镜子，他是生命的盐。不过真正的朋友实在不可多得。

"悲莫悲兮生别离，乐莫乐兮新相知。"①这儿可见生离死别是人生最悲惨的遭遇，心心相印是人生最快乐的境界。

在家庭里，父子、兄弟、姐妹等关系，完全基于血缘，他们本来也可以做朋友，但不一定个个是朋友。早在二三千年前，我们的民间诗人已经说过："虽有兄弟，不如友生。"②这说明气味不相投的兄弟，远不如披肝沥胆③的朋友更来得密切。

真是万事莫如吃饭难。富贵的人不必说，芸芸众生整天所忙的还不是为这一口饭。得之则生，不得则死，问题十分简单。一个人肯自动地把一口饭给你吃，的确不大容易。物质上可以帮忙的朋友既然不多，精神上能够相互沟通的更是凤毛麟角。尤其学术上，艺术上有特别成就的人，因为曲高和寡，所以不容易找到知音，在人海茫茫中显得十分寂寞。

人生世上，那位提携或教导你成功的人，当然算是知己；其次，在学问上互相鼓励，事业上彼此帮忙的人，当然也算是知己；再次，相知在师友之间，可以把毕生精力所换来的秘诀传授对方，让他做继承者的人，更可以说是知己。初出茅庐的青年，能够得到赏识你的上司，把你从广众中提拔出来已经不容易；在学问事业奋斗的过程中，能够找到三两个同志，彼此互相关照，使个人的力量扩大，这就很困难；在个人功成名就的时候，能够培植几个下一代的青年，作"火尽薪传"的打算，这就要看你个人识别的能力，甚至要看你的运气了。

现在让我们谈谈交友的方法。爱默生（R. W. Emerson）说："假如你要结交朋友，你本人须够朋友。"④老子也教人："将欲取之，必固与之。"当朋友有急需的时候，不等人家开口，你便自动给他帮忙，这是上策。其次，等人家开口后，才给他帮忙，这是中策。等到人家已经开口，你还斤斤计较地跟他漫天叫价，这是下策。

"与"的方面固然要相当豪爽，"取"的方面也应该识相，不要用尽人家的精力。譬如说，你的朋友本来有百分的能力，你仅请他帮你三分五分，至多不到十分，对方毫不费力，做起来够利落漂亮。另一方面，你的要求太高，弄到对方穷于应付，大家下不了台，到了你骂对方太刻薄、对方说你太苛求的时候，这就太不值得了。

交游广泛，固然是人生乐事，但朋友太多，你的时间和精神将大受影响，你的许多宝贵时间都给朋友的闲谈或应酬浪费了。为节省时间和精力起见，一个人须严戒滥交。反正泛泛之交会浪费你的时间和精力，对你的学问和事业是毫无益处。与其滥交一些酒肉朋友，不如随时严加警惕，只和少数有学问、有能力的人作道义之交。

老实说，朋友是可爱的。他是人生的镜子，他是生命的盐。不过真正的朋友实在不可多得，因为朋友是双方的，须看彼此的兴趣、能力、嗜好是否很接近。许多人白活了一辈子还交不到一个知己，所以"相识满天下，知心有几人"这两句话，到如今还有人传诵。

1955年元旦

注释：

① 悲莫悲兮生别离，乐莫乐兮新相知：出自屈原的《九歌》，意思为悲伤莫过于活生生的别离，快乐莫过于新相交的知己。

② 虽有兄弟，不如友生：出自《诗经·小雅》。友生，朋友。形容朋友的重要性。

③ 披肝沥胆：比喻开诚相见，也比喻极尽忠诚。

④ 假如你要结交朋友，你本人须够朋友：原文是 The only way to have a friend is to be one.

19 长得俏来才是俏

> 健康不但是一切幸福的基础,它简直是美的代名词。越健康的人便越美。要达到最美的程度,必须先维持最高度的健康。

好美是人类的天性,不过真正的美莫如自然。你瞧,天空变幻莫测的云霞,园中万紫千红的花卉,山上各种各色的鸟兽,海里奇形怪状的鱼虾,它们花纹的别致,颜色的鲜艳,没有一种经过人工的装饰,但没有一种不值得人们的赏玩。虽然世俗都主张,"人要衣装,佛要金装",不过化妆品无论多么香艳,服装无论多么新奇,首饰无论多么珠光宝气,这些仅能算是外表,不是实质。要找到实质的美,仅能诉诸自然,而自然的美,就是健美。

英国文豪洪德(J. Leigh Hunt)说:"健康是一切幸福的基础。"美国文豪爱默生也说:"健康是智慧的条件,是快乐的象征。"老实说，一个人宁愿过着清寒的生活而保持着健康，不愿意过着豪奢的生活而失掉健康。在平时，你还不觉得什么；当你病痛的时候，你这才知道健康是多么宝贵。美酒佳肴排在面前，你没法子享受；笙歌鼓乐近在身边，你也懒得倾听；名山胜水，你也不能去遨游。整天关在病院里，让大好时光虚度过去。到了这地步，你才明了健康是一切幸福的基础那句话，并不是凭空杜撰[①]的。

其实，健康不但是一切幸福的基础，它简直是美的代名词。越健康的人便越美。要达到最美的程度，必须先维持最高度的健康。

怎样才可以维持健康呢？这问题说来话长。用最简单的话来说，"安步可以当车，晚食可以当肉"[②]这句话，可说是维持健康的基本方法。

我们都知道运动的重要，因为运动使细胞新陈代谢的工作进行得更快，同时，使血液更见干净。不过各种运动，都是利弊参半，尤其剧烈的运动，一万次中只要有一次不小心，很可能会发生意外。只有散步，它才是有百利无一害。

与散步同等重要的，就是饮食。一般人以为能够享受三日一小宴，五日一大宴，是人生的乐事。其实，这种观念是错误的。一来，在大宴会里，不但饮食的种类太过复杂，而且分量实在太多，肚子消化不了。二来，宴会的时间太长，吃一顿饭，起码要两三个钟头，咸的、酸的、苦的、辣的，继续不断地往肚子里装，这未免使肚子的负担太过繁重。老实说，除必要的营养料，如牛奶、鸡蛋、蔬菜、水果外，简单清淡的饮食，远胜海味山珍。前者使消化力增强，后者使消化力衰退。因为病从口入，只要"口"这一关守得很严密，所有肠胃病都可一扫清光。

最后，保持健康的方法，就是除去烦恼，自信生理上心理上都很健全。"谁能相信自己很健康，便会健康。"(Who can believe himself well, he will be well.) 这句话并不是没有理由。现代医药虽十分发达，但高明的医生仍相信心理治疗，因为健全的心理对于生理是会发生意想不到的效力的。

健康是一切幸福的源泉，健康是美的先决条件。爱美的青年男女们，与其浪费金钱去买化妆品，不如先从加强和保持健康着手。俗语说："长得俏来才是俏，打扮俏来不算俏。"这倒是个真理，并不是开玩笑的。

1955 年 2 月 26 日深夜

注释：

① 杜撰 (zhuàn)：没有根据地编造，虚构。

② 晚食可以当肉：饿了以后才进食，虽然是粗茶淡饭，但其香甜可口胜过山珍海味。

20　响遏行云横碧落

> 除学校课程外，我们要特别注重音乐，琴书并重，松紧兼施，相信在音乐的美化净化下，我们每个公民的人格将更见高尚，生活更有意义。

谁家吹笛画楼中？断续声随断续风。
响遏行云横碧落，清和冷月到帘栊。[①]

——[唐]赵嘏《闻笛》

人类没有发明文字以前，早就会说话，尤其会唱歌。终年辛苦的工人，当他们胼手胝足[②]地搬运笨重的木头或石子的时候，他们自然会哼出"吭唷""吭唷"的声音。在较大规模的场合里，做工头的人，以洪亮的嗓子唱出一两句，其余的工人自动地跟着唱和。彼起此落，一步紧接一步。虽然在劳动的过程中，他们会弄到汗流浃背，但是，经过一段最简单的唱和后，他们的精神似乎更舒畅，步伐似乎更轻松。相反的，假如他们老是低着头，闷着气，继续不断地苦干，他们的工作效率，很可能会降低一半。

同样的，在山上砍柴、采桑、采茶的农村男女，在荒草茫茫、白杨萧萧的环境里工作，心情多少是不佳。为振奋精神、提高工作情绪起见，他们偶尔会引吭高歌。不料这种由衷的原始歌曲，引起散处山上同伴的共鸣，此唱彼和，不停不歇。这样一来，大家壮了胆量，不怕森林里的毒蛇猛兽；同时也抖擞了精神，借工作的机会，找到异性的安慰。

其实，中国古代的大教育家早就知道音乐的重要。在孔门的六艺里，音乐和体育两科的总和，比较后代的只重读本、写作和数学的三科制度大得多。现代医学家教人延年益寿的办法，最重要的是放松你的神经，而放松神经的关键，主要的是靠音乐。假如你自己懂得玩一两种乐器，那是再好不过；不然，听听收音机、电唱机，也可以忘怀得失。最后，当你既不会演奏，又没有收音机、电唱机的设备的时候，你不妨在傍晚洗澡的时候，鼓足气力，乱唱一场，把一天来所受的冤屈闷气，随着歌声全部吐出来。

音乐不但是调剂身心最有效的手段，而且是结交朋友最良好的办法。普通社会上所谓朋友，多数是虚伪的，表面上称兄道弟，背后往往会飞短流长，听了使人颇不舒服。音乐则不然。它是人类的纯正的心声，圣洁的灵魂。社会上可以有许多虚伪的礼节，但你怎样也找不到虚伪的音乐。真正懂得音乐的人，他的心灵永远是愉快的，生活永远是充实的。

我们青年人不能整天用功，因为这不但有害身体，而且使精神得不到放松的机会。在这当儿，我们希望音乐界的朋友，牺牲一些时间和精神，起来领导。无论音乐也好，声乐也好，只要有关于健康的文娱，我们应该予以热烈地支持。

的确，有的时候千言万语，远不如演奏一首曲，高唱一首歌。在皓月当空的深夜，"长笛一声人倚楼"，这是多么美妙的景象。在清风和煦的薄暮，当你从野餐会整装归来的时候，忽听隔岸的歌声，回头一看，见不到半个影子，"曲终人不见，江上数峰青"，像这么富有诗情画意的环境，主要的是得力于音乐。

因此，除学校课程外，我们要特别注重音乐，琴书并重，松紧兼施，相信在音乐的美化净化下，我们每个公民的人格将更见高尚，生活更有意义。

1959年7月19日

注释：

① 响遏(è)行云横碧落，清和冷月到帘栊：只觉得笛音高亢，响遏行云；笛音清越，有如冷月临窗。赵嘏(gǔ)的《闻笛》全诗是"谁家吹笛画楼中？断续声随断续风。响遏行云横碧落，清和冷月到帘栊。兴来三弄有桓子，赋就一篇怀马融。曲罢不知人在否，余音嘹亮尚飘空"。

② 胼(pián)手胝(zhī)足：胼胝，茧子。手脚上磨出老茧。形容经常地辛勤劳动。

21　花木成蹊手自栽

> 他生在那个时代，已经充分了解劳工的地位，所以在可能范围内，他尽量用自己的劳力来谋生，不占人家半点便宜。事实上，劳动之后，得到片刻的休息，那种休息是特别有滋味。

假如你要我在中国历史上找个大政治家兼大文豪的人物，我无疑地要先提到王安石。

王安石一生虽努力于文章和事业，但他的私人生活却很有风趣。当他在金陵闲居时写过这么一首诗：

　　茅檐常扫净无苔，花木成蹊①手自栽。
　　一水护田将绿绕，两山排闼送青来②。

在这首诗里，你可以体会到他的苦心。茅檐下本来是乱七八糟，东边一堆野草，西边一堆垃圾，只因勤于洗刷，所以干净到没有青苔。普通有社会地位的人，花木的种植工作都留给家里的仆人去干，自己从来不去打理，任他花开花谢，木荣木枯，一点也不留心。可是王安石本人对于花木的种植，完全由自己动手，所以十年后，花木成荫，而花间的空地，因为他朝夕勤于灌溉，不知不觉间造成一条小径。

我对王安石这首诗却另有一种看法。我不大注意下两句怎样欣赏周遭的景物，远山近水的情调，我着重上两句怎样辛勤洗刷，怎样动手栽种。换句话说，在这两句诗里，以推翻不合理的旧制度为职业的王安石，早已提出并且实行"劳动神圣"的口号。

本来儒家是维持现状，拥护统治阶级的，这种办法一般老百姓非常看不顺眼。因此当孔子叫他的得意门生子路去询问道路的时候，那位老粗的农民很不客气地教训他一顿，说："四体不勤，五谷不分，孰为夫子？"[3]说时，心里的抑郁不平之气，恨不得都往子路身上吐。

王安石生在宋朝，本身是个宰相，又是个大文豪，普通没有修养的人如处在他的地位，一定会踌躇满志。但他不然，他虽有五六十个亲戚朋友要靠他吃饭，但他个人却自奉菲薄，最难得的是他生在那个时代，已经充分了解劳工的地位，所以在可能范围内，他尽量用自己的劳力来谋生，不占人家半点便宜。事实上，劳动之后，得到片刻的休息，那种休息是特别有滋味。就像"茅檐常扫净无苔，花木成蹊手自栽"这两句诗，它们充分证明王安石不是乱喊口号，而是以实际的劳力来找寻生活的真正乐趣。

在社会主义国家里，没有专门工作或专门享乐的阶级之分。换句话说，谁都要工作，谁都要学习。工作和学习是分不开的，只有这样，工人对于他们的工作才觉得有兴趣，同时因为他们对工作有兴趣，所以效率增加，成绩卓著。工作之暇，他们还能够从事文娱：尽情欢乐，尽情歌唱，尽情舞蹈。相比较在旧社会里，有的人拼命享乐，有的人拼命工作；有的人胀死，有的人饿死；有的人闲得要命，有的人忙得要命……生活方式的差距非常大。

就我个人而论，35年前，我在故乡念王安石这首诗的时候，虽然过眼成诵，但诗里的真意义并不大明白，直到后来自己在社会服务，同时，阅读一些经济理论及社会主义的书籍后，这才能够体会出"花木成蹊手自栽"的真谛。

1955年5月8日深夜

注释：

① 蹊：小路。

② 一水护田将绿绕，两山排闼(tà)送青来：庭院外一条小河护卫着农田，把绿色的田地环绕，两座青山推开门，送来青翠的山色。

③ 四体不勤，五谷不分，孰为夫子：四体，指人的两手两足；五谷，通常指稻(dào)、黍(shǔ)、稷(jì)即粟、麦(mài)、菽(shū)即豆类的总称。夫子，旧时对学者的尊称。四体不勤，五谷不分，指不参加劳动，不能辨别五谷。形容脱离生产劳动，缺乏生产知识。

22　万物静观皆自得

> "静观"不是逃避事实,而是有计划地做"宁静"的准备。到了心平气和的时候,一个人的精神集中,意志如神,凡事比较别人总看得深刻些。

闲来无事不从容,睡觉东窗日已红。
万物静观皆自得,四时佳兴与人同。①

——[宋]程颢《偶成》

以上四句出自宋朝程颢(程明道)的诗。最重要的一句"万物静观皆自得"颇值得我们细心玩味。

自都市发达、人口集中后,"静"这个字差不多要销声匿迹了。都市的特色是繁华、热闹、嘈杂、混乱。除富商巨贾、达官显宦外,普通中等以下的家庭,住的是拥挤的陋室,行的是沙丁鱼似的公共汽车,食的是万头攒动的公共食堂。至于办公的地方,有的是轧轧轧的打字机、计算机、电话铃的声音。假如在工厂工作,那隆隆的马达及上下移动的机器的声音,不但震耳欲聋,而且使人觉得又单调又烦腻。

　　本来人类是环境的产物,在一种环境下,人类的反应是这样;换了一个环境,他的反应是那样。孔子曾说:"知者乐水,仁者乐山。知者动,仁者静。知者乐,仁者寿。"撇开"知者"和"仁者"这些名词不谈,我们知道住在山上的人多数爱静,因为爱静,所以他享尽天年②。住在海滨的人多数爱动,因为爱动,所以他的生活比较丰富,享乐的机会也比较住在城里的人多了几倍。

　　"静观"的人一定恬淡寡欲的;一个人能够恬淡寡欲,便不会热衷③。庄子就是这么一个人。据《史记》的记载,楚威王听说庄子的能力很强,特地派人用许多礼物送他,请他答应做宰相。假如别的人处在这地位,难免高兴得连眼泪也流出来。可是,庄子却拒绝了。假如他平时对于"静观"的功夫做得不够,我相信他绝不会这么恬淡寡欲。

　　我常觉得诸葛亮给他儿子那封信里的两句话,"非淡泊无以明志,非宁静无以致远",是他一生最得力的处世南针。生活不够淡泊的人,整天争名夺利,征逐酒色财气,久而久之,把所有抱负都放弃了。态度不够宁静的人,凡事只见个皮相,便沾沾自喜;这种人急于近功,绝没有比较远大的计划。诸葛亮爱子心切,所以他才把平生最得力的秘诀传授给儿子,希望他不至误入歧途。

"静观"不是逃避事实，而是有计划地做"宁静"的准备。到了心平气和的时候，一个人的精神集中，意志如神，凡事比较别人总看得深刻些。事实上，真正能够"静观"的人，他心空如明镜。外物的美丑妍媸④，——可在镜里反映出来。假如一个人的心不够宁静，甚至有些浮动，那么这好像一面蒙尘的镜，摇来晃去，外物再也看不清楚了。

宁静的心情是养生的秘诀。它可以益智，可以延年。整天纷纷扰扰地胡思乱想，白天固疲惫不堪，到了晚上照样不能安眠。这种生活，正是虽生之日，犹死之年。能静观的人，一定能达观，一个人能够把事物的本末先后、表里精粗、是非利害都看透了，他哪里还肯为芝麻大的事情去跟人争执呢？

由环境的宁静，造成心情的宁静；由心情的宁静，把周遭的景物也一一美化了。只有在这情形下，对任何事物，才可尝到优游自得的滋味。

1955年2月6日清晨

注释：

① 闲来无事不从容，睡觉东窗日已红。万物静观皆自得，四时佳兴与人同：心情闲静安适，做什么事情都不慌不忙的。一觉醒来，红日已高照东窗了。静观万物，都可以得到自然的乐趣，人们对一年四季中美妙风光

的兴致都是一样的。

此七言律诗的后四句为"道通天地有形外,思入风云变态中。富贵不淫贫贱乐,男儿到此是豪雄"。

②天年:指人的自然寿命。

③热衷:急切盼望得到(个人的地位或利益等)。

④妍(yán)媸(chī):妍,美丽;媸,相貌丑,跟妍相对。

23　又得浮生半日闲

> 一个人须懂得利用闲暇来行进德修业、锻炼体魄等有益于身心的事情，不然，"群居终日，言不及义"，或者"饱食终日，无所用心"，闲暇反而变成累赘。

在《功名不上懒人头》那篇短文里，我劝年轻人应该用功，现在却提出这么一个题目:《又得浮生半日闲》，强调"闲"的重要。表面上看来，我好像是前后矛盾；事实上，二者是有联系性，一点也不矛盾。

在办事或治学的人的字典里，"懒"字不可有，"闲"字不可无。"懒"字表示完全消极，"闲"字却带积极的意思。一来平素神经过分紧张，偶尔找半天的闲暇，把神经松弛一下，这对于身心的健康都有益处。二来在公司办理例行公务的人，差不多等于一架会说话的机器，忙了一天，并不会增进什么经验或知识。这样的人极需要半天的闲暇，让他的脑筋从昏迷的状态中苏醒过来。经过休养和调整，第二天上班时，他更能够应付各种困难的问题。

俗语说："天下本无事，庸人自扰之。"这句话实在很有道理。一般庸人多是自作聪明，把小事变成大事，纷纷扰扰，毫无宁日。他们应该尽量减少无事忙，多留一点闲工夫来沉思默想，或者阅览一些增益见闻的书籍，说不定可以除却许多纠纷。

古人所谓"清夜自思""扪心自问"，这些事情绝不是一天忙到晚的人所能够做得到。一般忙人，根本没有思维的工夫，他们的办法，就是干、干、干，到了事情出了岔子，然后怨天尤人，把自己应负的责任推得一干二净。假如他们真正能够抽出一点时间来检讨是非得失，就能减少许多不必要的纠纷。

一个人无论怎么忙，他应该懂得忙里偷闲，尤其政治家和实业家，他们整天忙着料理事务、批阅文件、订立计划、主持会议、接见宾客，简直是忙得不可开交。但是，第一流的政治家，无论工作怎么忙碌，他总懂得忙里偷闲地从事修养。

英国名相丘吉尔，最懂得忙里偷闲。他每天要办理很多事情，但他又能够抽出一点空闲的时间来假寐，因为从假寐醒来的时候，精神兴奋百倍。事实上，只有在兴高采烈的心情下,一个人对于任何事情都发生浓厚的兴趣,同时因为兴趣的浓厚,他做什么事情都有心得。无怪他对于文学、军事、政治、外交、绘画等,样样都在行。他到了81岁,才开始学习雕刻,这说明忙里偷闲的人是最懂得享受人生。

  一个人须懂得利用闲暇来行进德修业、锻炼体魄等有益于身心的事情,不然,"群居终日,言不及义"[①],或者"饱食终日,无所用心"[②],闲暇反而变成累赘。到了一个人要费更大的精力、更多的心思来做"无聊的消遣"的时候,闲暇的意义完全失掉了。

  生活在繁华的都市,"又得浮生半日闲"是很不容易的事情。我们除每天忙里偷闲,做比较有意义的工作外,每星期至少须有半天闲工夫,因为闲暇能善为利用,它是百利无一害。

1955年5月22日深夜

注释:
 ① 群居终日,言不及义:比喻整天成群地聚在一起,不讲正经事。
 ② 饱食终日,无所用心:比喻整天吃饱了饭,什么也不思考。

24　乡音无改鬓毛衰

> 健全的母语教育，使人有表情达意的良好工具，同时，使人有立身处世的技能。

"乡音"的另一名称是"母舌"或"母语"（Mother Tongue）。一个婴孩在慈爱的母亲的抚育下，心里非常愉快，模仿的本能又极强烈。从他一岁左右刚学话的时候起，母亲怎么说，他也跟着怎么说。到了四五岁生日的时候，他已经能够自由运用各种语法和语气了。他的字汇和成语天天在增加。除非在十岁以前，把他换到完全不同的另一环境、另一地方，强迫他从头学习另一国语或方言，他的浓厚的乡音是永远不会改变的。

友人刘攻芸先生非常推崇韩素音女士的英文学造诣。他说："韩素音的英文才够英国的味儿。"但是韩素音本人说："我之所以能够写得一手英文，为的是得力于中文。"这话并不是危言耸听，而是有事实的根据。蒋彝先生二十年来靠英文谋生，也靠英文成名。在他所发表的二十种英文著作中，除小部分以"哑行者"的名义撰述各地的游记外，比较充实的著作不但以中文材料做背景，而且根本上是用英文来讨论中国的书法和美术。此外，他书中的插图是纯粹中国的笔调，这对于外国的读者不消说有新鲜的感觉。

我固然注意"乡音"或母语的重要性，但我不反对人家学习外国语。我所争的就是韩文公所提出的"闻道有先后，术业有专攻"[1]这一点。换句话说，华人的子弟须先精通中文，等到行有余力，才兼治英文。假如华人的子弟先学习英文，甚至把中文置之脑后，这不但使他见弃于高明的外国人，而且使他在华洋杂处的社会里不知所措。

提到学习"母语"问题，我们不禁会想到瑞士。瑞士的人种很复杂，它的一切公文是用德、法、意三种文字写成的。在法律上，任何人都得享受平等待遇。每一民族都有自己的方言学校；儿童把母语读通后，便开始学习第二、第三，甚至第四种语文。对外政令统一，对内彼此平等，所以瑞士的社会秩序的良好，在欧洲可以说首屈一指。

中国有句俗语："子不嫌母丑，犬不厌家贫。"这些话最能道出中国文化的伟大，中国民风的醇厚。

离开故乡三十多年了。我承认我的故乡是个穷乡僻壤，我也承认我的故乡是个风气闭塞、文化落后的地方。但故乡赐我以健康的体魄，故乡赋我以善良的心灵，故乡更给我以百折不挠②的意志、积极乐观的精神。这些东西是我出而问世的唯一可靠的本钱。

"乡音无改鬓毛衰。"③任何人朗读这句诗的时候，应该引以为荣，因为无情的光阴虽然一天一天催人衰老，但浓厚的"乡音"却屹立不动，一点也不会变更。尤其健全的母语教育，使人有表情达意的良好工具，同时，使人有立身处世的技能。本来教育是发挥本能的手段，人类的良知良能，因教育得法而能够充分发挥，教育的目的便算达到。不然削足适履④，尽量贬抑"母语"，藐视"乡音"，这种办法我却不敢领教。

1955 年 9 月 4 日于东海酒店

注释：

① 闻道有先后，术业有专攻：知道道理有先有后，技能学业各有专门研究。

② 百折不挠（náo）：折，挫折；挠，屈服。形容意志坚强，无论受到多少挫折，都不屈服。

③ 乡音无改鬓毛衰：衰，古音读 cuī，指人老了鬓发疏落变白。本句意思是人虽然老了，但乡音却没有改变。

④ 削足适履（lǚ）：履，鞋子。为了要穿上鞋子而把脚切去一块。比喻不恰当地迁就，勉强凑合。

25　一将功成万骨枯

> 战争是可诅咒的,它拆散人家的父母、兄弟、妻儿。它使历史上有价值的建筑物化为灰烬,它把人类纯良的天性压制下去,把他们好勇斗狠的兽性发挥出来。参加打仗的人,十去九不回。

泽国江山入战图,生民何计入樵苏。
凭君莫话封侯事,一将功成万骨枯。[①]
　　　　　——[唐]曹松《己亥岁》

当我高声诵读唐人这首诗的时候,我的眼前忽然一阵昏黑,接着,两只耳朵嗡嗡作响,全身毛发倒竖起来。我记得报载第一枚原子弹从天空扔下来,12平方公里内的房屋和人民全部毁灭。

由于武器的进步,都市的发展,人口的增加,"英雄"的行情扶摇直上。在弓箭时代,一个将军的代价是"万"名白骨。在枪炮时代,将军或总司令的代价,起码涨到100倍。第一次世界大战，死亡的兵士1300万人，死伤的平民3300多万人，光是这两笔数字，死伤总数已达4600万人，而孤儿、寡妇、俘虏、难民还不算在内。平均一个将军的代价是百万生灵。假如照目前的武器及人口集中情形而论，海、陆、空上将的代价显然看涨。

远在三四十年前，中国的土匪很多，官方派兵去围剿，土匪招架不住，于是向政府投诚，改为官兵；过了不久，官兵因粮尽饷绝，又纷纷跑去当土匪。一把毛瑟枪在手，随时可当官兵，也随时可做土匪，兵匪不分，吃亏的就是老百姓。

由于社会组织的严密，法律权威的提高，军政大员言出法随。他们要人民打仗，人民不能不打仗。虽然每次打仗都有堂皇的理由；但政治一变，由敌国变成友邦的时候，又有一套更漂亮动听的理由。我常说，那些搞军事、政治、经济、外交、宣传的人，至少须自备一部正反两用的辞典，赞成某种政策时，用正面的理论；反对某种政策时，用的是反面的理论。是正是反，决定政策的人，永远不会错的，而错误的责任，须由人民负担，一切牺牲，也由人民承当。

自卫的战争还是情有可原，穷兵黩武[②]地向外侵略，却是罪不容诛。在古战场上作冤鬼的人，真是"天地为愁，草木凄悲。吊祭不至，精魂何依"。他们死得毫无价值，除以骨肉头颅替各级将领做垫脚石外，他们得不到半点好处。

话又说回来，人民的个别反战不会发生效力，最重要的是把世界各国的反战人民组织起来,造成坚强无比的和平堡垒。科学的发明应充分用来做和平用途,使全世界人民的生活享受能够提高,然后有余力做文化的交流。

战争是可诅咒的,它拆散人家的父母、兄弟、妻儿。它使历史上有价值的建筑物化为灰烬,它把人类纯良的天性压制下去,把他们好勇斗狠的兽性发挥出来。参加打仗的人,十去九不回。在古代妇女可以免兵役,但在男女平等的社会,妇女也可以上前线,所以她们仍旧逃避不了战争的迫害。

我们只要细心思考"一将功成万骨枯"的名句,反战的情绪不禁油然而生。在这种情绪下,谁要牵着我们的鼻子发动侵略的战争,恐怕没有那么容易了。

1955年3月13日清晨

注释:

① 泽国江山入战图,生民何计入樵苏。凭君莫话封侯事,一将功成万骨枯:泽国,指长江以南的地区;樵苏,砍柴割草,泛指艰苦的生活;封侯,古代将帅战争立功可以升官。意思是一片河山都绘入战图,百姓只求能砍柴割草度日,如今连这种所谓的快乐也不能得到。请你不要再提封侯的话了,一个将领的成功要牺牲多少士卒的生命啊!

② 穷兵黩(dú)武:黩武,滥用武力。使用全部武力,任意发动侵略战争。

26　安得广厦千万间

> 只因杜甫一辈子吃了没有钱的亏,弄得他无家可归,仅住在破陋的茅屋,又偏遭风雨,所以他才发个宏愿,要建筑"广厦千万间"。

生活在繁华的都市里,一个人整天忙到晚,为的是怎样解决衣食住行这些琐碎问题。一般说来,行的问题比较容易解决,有钱的坐小车,没钱的坐大车(公共汽车),虽然大车沿途要停留,不如小车的直截了当,但大车仍旧能够把你送到目的地,而路头路尾须多走几分钟,这对于你的健康不但没有妨碍,反而有点益处。

食的问题在都市也很随便。久居南洋的人对于吃这问题尤其不大考究,只要有故乡风味,连路边也可以坐下去,大家吃得津津有味。

衣的问题在新加坡也很马虎。在新加坡除少数人要追求时尚外，普通妇女可以穿着便装满街跑。至于男人，普通所谓"白领阶层"早已连领带也不结，仅穿一件衬衫到处走动了。

衣、食、行三者都容易应付，剩下只有住这个问题最伤脑筋。

就新加坡而论，寸金尺土，屋租非常昂贵。普通住屋已经很难找，便利往来旅客的旅店，更是供不应求。记得1937年8月20日，我带着一家人从北京日军的铁蹄下逃出来的时候，费了14个钟头才抵达天津。好容易才找到一间破烂不堪的旅店。行李刚刚放下，倾盆大雨便继续不断地漏进房里。就在那时候，我觉得杜甫的《茅屋为秋风所破歌》饶有趣味，尤其"安得广厦千万间，大庇天下寒士俱欢颜"[①]那句，仿佛是专门写给我看的。

人口密集的都市，生病的人特别多。一个人生了病，当然要找医生。私人医生索价高，只有中上家庭才有资格光顾。中下家庭因为经济关系，无力光顾私人医生，他们只好跑到政府医院去求医。政府医院上门求诊的病人特别多，医生还没来，候诊室早已挤满了人。等了半天，才能够见到医生。医生给病人弄得头昏脑涨，一面听病人说病情，一面手不停地挥开药方。病人拿到药方后，跑到药房去取药，药房里又是挤满了人，又得等上半天才能够拿到药。生了一点毛病，要到政府医院看病，至少须半天工夫，所以许多穷人患了小病多是忍气吞声，硬着头皮去工作，直到病入膏肓[②]的时候，才由家人送到政府医院去留医。

"安得广厦千万间"这句诗,真是掷地作金声。它说明我们的诗圣的抱负不凡,他绝不自私,只求大公;宁愿牺牲小我,以便完成大我。它又说明,世界上只有穷人才能够最了解穷人,最能够帮助穷人。

只因杜甫一辈子吃了没有钱的亏,弄得他无家可归,仅住在破陋的茅屋,又偏遭风雨,所以他才发个宏愿,要建筑"广厦千万间"。可惜"广厦千万间"的上边加着"安得"两字,这又证明诗圣仅剩下幻想,和事实永远保持相当的距离。

注释:

①安得广厦千万间,大庇天下寒士俱欢颜:取自杜甫诗《茅屋为秋风所破歌》,意思是怎么才能得到千万间宽敞高大的房子,普遍地庇覆天下间贫寒的读书人,让他们个个都开颜欢笑?

②病入膏肓(huāng):指疾病重到无法医治的地步。

27　天生我材必有用

> 真正有学问的人,他对于自己的前途是有绝对的信心的。不论环境的顺逆,机会的好坏,他还是奋勇直前地按照自己的计划来进行。

一个人妄自尊大固然没有必要,妄自菲薄也是多余。妄自尊大,往往引人讨厌;妄自菲薄,也时常被人可怜。本着"丈夫不肯受人怜"的观念,一个有相当自尊心的人,怎能给人家可怜?

本来一个人的学问的深浅,能力的高低,完全要看个人的天才和努力来决定。天分高,而又肯拼命用功的人,他的学问一定很充实,能力一定很坚强,遇事自己总有充分的把握。另一方面,一个人是否能够得到适当的机会来表现自己的学问和能力,这还须看环境的顺逆而定。

但是,真正有学问的人,他对于自己的前途是有绝对的信心的。不论环境的顺逆，机会的好坏，他还是奋勇直前地按照自己的计划来进行。我行我素，心安理得，世俗的毁誉是非，他根本不放在眼内。

唐朝的李白，是个聪明绝顶的大诗人。他的性格倜傥①不羁，行为相当浪漫。虽然如此，他的抱负却相当高，同代里趋炎附势②、跑门路、钻狗洞的人，他一概看不起。因此，在他的名作《将进酒》里，他以极豪放的心情，大声喝道："天生我材必有用，千金散尽还复来。"

其实"天生我材必有用"，并不是酒后狂言，它只证明我们的大诗人对于他自己的前途很有信心罢了。须知一个人必须有自信心，他这才敢努力往前干；只要肯干，前途才铺着光明的大道。假如信心消失，自己不肯努力，那么前途一定十分黯淡。

宗教家教人，开宗明义第一章，就是一个"信"字。因为有信仰而后有力量，宗教家的虔诚，就是他一切力量的源泉。

英国大文豪约翰生（Samuel Johnson, 1709—1784）说得好："自信是伟大事业的先决条件。"（Self-confidence is the first requisite to great undertakings.）这话一点也不错。约翰生是个文人，他不是叱咤风云的名将，他也不是运筹帷幄的谋士，他更不是富可敌国的大资本家，所以他没有经营大事业。但他一生有件事值得自豪，因为他算是第一位编纂英文字典（A

Dictionary of the English Language)的人。当他要进行这伟大计划的时候,他曾前往伦敦拜见一个文人。他在会客室里坐了几个钟头,始终得不到那位文人的青睐。十几年之后,他的英文字典居然大功告成,约翰生变成伦敦的风云人物。就在这时候,十几年前想见而见不到的社会文人,准备送他一笔钱,他毫不考虑地原封不动送回去。你想,在十八世纪的英国,交通那么不方便,公共图书馆既不发达,他个人又贫病交加,假如他没有自信心,他哪里会下个决心,从事编纂英文字典的伟举?只因他具备百折不挠的自信心,继续不断地往前干,结果,把字典编纂成功,在英国文学史上写一新页。

"天生我材必有用"这句话是教人应有自信心。事实上,一个人有了自信心,这才不至妄自菲薄或妄自尊大了。

1955 年 9 月 27 日清晨

注释:

① 倜(tì)傥(tǎng):洒脱,不拘束。
② 趋炎附势:奉承依附有权有势的人。

28　人到无求品自高

> 尽人事,听天命,对于任何事业,都要从工作的本身找到乐趣,既不为名,又不为利,这才能够坦坦荡荡地培养浩然之气。

人和人相处,免不了要发生"取"和"与"的行为。第一流人物是"与"多于"取"。在可能范围内,尽量给人以种种方便。孔子的"诲人不倦",纯粹注重"与"这方面,因为"与"人越多,他所"取"的也越多。你瞧,在两千五百多年前,交通多么不方便,而孔子在杏坛设教的时候,居然有那么多的学生,这还不是"诲人不倦"的精神上的收获?

老子更是懂得斤斤计较的人物。他说:"将欲取之,必固与之。"这充分说明,真正要"取",就得先"与";所"与"越多,所"取"也越多。根据"既以与人己愈多"的理论,多"与"比较多"取"更为有利。

中等人物，对于"取"和"与"的行为比较平衡，他是"一点不占人家的便宜，一点也不给人家占便宜"。欧美社会所流行的"AA制"（Go Dutch），多少是受他们的权利义务均等理论的影响。

下流人物，只懂得"取"，不懂得"与"。在他们的心目中，以为这是最聪明最占便宜的办法，不知他们所付的代价比较任何人都大。

俗语说："人为财死，鸟为食亡。"这句话把人类贪多务得的心理所造成的恶果完全道破。鸟儿如不贪食，它们被捕的机会可以说是减去99%。人们如不贪财，他们当然会安分守己，过着返璞归真的生活。哪里还会丧尽天良，干出"谋财害命"或"卖友""卖国"的勾当？

读者也许会笑我太落后。我平素看人，最注重他的私德。一个人的私生活十分严肃，"临财毋苟取，临难无苟免"，这才可以跟他谈论治国平天下的大事。假如他的私生活一塌糊涂，酒、色、财、气，一应俱全，到了入不敷出的时候，他难免要昧着良心，干出种种不可告人的事情了。

"我去求人六月霜"这句话很有道理。当你向人家有所求的时候，你已有所准备，人家是毫无准备；你可以大开海口，人家当然不会有求必应。的确，求人实在不容易。除了莫逆之交外，你如向普通朋友开口借钱或者求事，恐怕你也是想踏进他的大门而又不敢进去，想开口而又不敢老老实实地说出来吧。

中国古代有两个人：一个是黔娄①，另一个是陶渊明。黔娄穷得要命，饿得半死，可是他绝对不争名逐利。一个人的态度那么坚决，神志那么清明，试问谁还能够奈何得他？陶渊明不为五斗米折腰，只因他决心安贫乐道，才能够思想超脱，写出天地间的至文。

我并不是教人消极，相反地，我是教人须永远积极乐观。不过我有个条件，就是私人生活须力求严肃，不受酒、色、财、气支配。尽人事，听天命，对于任何事业，都要从工作的本身找到乐趣，既不为名，又不为利，这才能够坦坦荡荡地培养浩然之气。事实上，人到"无求"的地步，他绝对不会随便向人低头了。竖起脊梁，挺起胸膛，仰首伸眉，讨论天下事，得失荣辱，全不放在心里，一个人的修养达到这田地，还怕品格不会高吗？

1955 年 5 月 16 日深夜

注释：

① 黔 (qián) 娄 (lóu)：战国时齐国隐士。

For the New Youth

Preface

In the summer of 1953, I visited the picturesque Penang with my wife and son, Liang. Thanks to my dear friend, Dai Yunfeng, we had the luxury of staying in a villa atop Penang Hill and in another on the bays of Tanjong Bungah, both of which Yunfeng borrowed for us from his friends. We spent our week in Penang sightseeing and it released all the tension I had built up over the years.

It was a short trip of no more than thirteen days, but my wife had gained five pounds, while my son had made many new friends along the way. When we reached home, I asked my wife if she enjoyed the thrills of travel. She responded with much enthusiasm and even offered to write an essay recollecting the delightfulness and joys that travel brings for her. However, eighteen months passed since the trip and she was not yet done with the travelogue she had earnestly planned to write. I understand how onerous housekeeping can get; a housewife, as educated as she can be, would barely have the mood for writing after a draining day of household chores, let alone years. Therefore, I did not rush her and instead took to writing the travelogue myself.

Ever since the publication of the essay, my passion for writing was re-ignited and I started to write more, producing articles after articles. There was once when I had a terrible stomach upset after eating something wrong. It stopped me from writing for two days, but when I recovered slightly on the third day, I pulled myself together and finished what I wanted to write after staying up the entire night to do it. As from small increments comes abundance, the book was finally completed in May, around five months after starting on it last Christmas.

The issues of the youths only rose to prominence after the May Fourth Movement. What are the issues of the youths, you may ask? These issues, long story short, included issues surrounding education, revolution, relationships, careers and self-cultivation. However, not all of these are applicable in the Singaporean context. For one, as a colony of Britain that is about to gain partial self-governance in April this year, most Singaporean adopt a more cautionary attitude and steer clear from even the very mention of "politics"; lofty ideals and talks of revolutions are far beyond their concerns. Similar to that are the concerns of love and careers – the social atmosphere here is a lot more open, the children study in co-ed schools, and before the founding of Nanyang University, the highest institutes of learning for the Chinese are mostly secondary schools. At such a tender age, they are provided for by the parents and older siblings in terms of their daily needs – what other problems of immediate concern do they face, aside from their education and self-cultivation? Also, besides these two issues, youths should also take into account their extra-curricular activities.

With regard to education and studying, I have actually talked in brief about my personal experiences once in my book *40 Years of Reflection*, and another in my essay *On Strategies in Scholarship*; I will therefore not discuss these issues in my current book. Instead, I will focus more on the conduct and cultivation of the youths today.

The pioneers of scientific socialism told us that "it is not the consciousness of men that determines their existence but their social existence that determines their consciousness." Therefore, it is necessary for youths with ambitions to choose, adapt and even make full use of the environment that they are in.

In the past years, I have been encouraging the youths to do these three things: "stay healthy, learn earnestly, and love one another." Later, I read in the newspapers that the advisors in China also encourage the youths to take note of three things: "stay healthy, study hard, and work diligently." Such simple and relatable goals are ones that we can all agree in one accord. It is important to know that health is the source of all happiness, as well as our most reliable capital. With health, there will be joy all day long; without health, life will be drowned with sorrow. I hope every ambitious youth will put in rigorous effort to build a body of steel, so they can shoulder the responsibilities that the society have entrusted to them.

Studying and working are indivisible in the first place. Generally speaking, studying and working are the same as learning. We ought to keep learning all our life; even so, we will realise that there is no end to learning. You see, even if one learns tirelessly, there is only so much that he or she can learn. Imagine one always thinks that the grass is greener in other pastures and always learn by fits and starts; his or her achievement will be greatly limited.

When it comes to teaching, the great sages of every culture all emphasize upon the foundation of learning. Before one engages in learning, he or she must have a right heart and a sincere will. That is why I am more than willing to repeatedly discuss topics like "ambition", "planning", "preparation", and "diligence". A youth who is determined to learn should have a pure motivation and good intention, just as an artist must first prepare a spotless plain paper. Otherwise, if one has the wrong understanding, erratic perspective, arrogant attitude, turning every learning into fuel for vices, and craves for fame and wealth; not only will this person be useless to the nation and society, he or she may even become a stumbling block to the advancement of the generation.

The youths born to this time must take it upon themselves to guard the peace of the world because nuclear weapons are progressing by leap and bound each day. Unless the world is in peace, our descendants will inevitably be reduced to cannon fodder and the civilisation will be endangered.

I have high expectations of youths, that is why I articulated all that I know without reserve. The good thing about this book is that it is not a sermon; I am merely sharing my perspectives through my writings on the issues that the youths are concerned with but are clueless about. Apart from conveying principles, I also tried my best to use metaphors and allegories, hoping to make it easier for the youth to understand, and at the same time, enhance the reading experience.

As for the title of the essays, I use idioms for some, and poetic verses for the others. I have no intention of parading my learning; I use them because I truly feel that many Chinese idioms and verses are highly refined, and they are worth reading again and again. For instance, "On Making Friends" is a title which primary and secondary school students can write about. I use "There Is No Greater Joy Than Making New Friends" from Songs of Chu as my title; this may have a more profound meaning in terms of literary relations. Or "On Anti-War" is a title which professors or newspaper editors can write about, but the great Russian novelist, Leo Tolstoy, written a four-volume novel with the title *War and Peace.* As for me, I used a famous verse of a Tang poem, "A General Glory, Ten Thousands Bodies" as the title and written an essay. Unfortunately, I am less well-read and lack experience; I really wanted to imitate Tolstoy and turn this simple topic into an extensive work.

This book only represents my personal views on the issues of self-cultivation with regard to the youths. It can be used for discussions outside the classroom. I know youths are most straightforward and sincere, so if there is anything wrong with what I have written, I hope the youths in different places will point it out to me unreservedly.

Written in Singapore in the late night of 9 September 1955,
Lien Shih Sheng

Contents

1	Planning for the year ahead in spring	101
2	Carrying dry rations when full, an umbrella on a clear day	105
3	It is all owed to the wellspring, its running water	109
4	Making a name for yourself by becoming an expert in one area	113
5	Who can still study when he is old	117
6	The mansion is windswept as a mountain storm approaches	121
7	The waves of the Yangtze River surge ever forward	125
8	Disputes come from talking too much	129
9	Enmity should be resolved, not engendered	132
10	A moment of misstep, an eternity of regret	136
11	Flowers not yet fully to blossom, the moon not yet full	140
12	Fame will not crown the lazy head	144
13	The grass is always greener on the other side	147
14	A performance is "seven parts gong and three parts song"	150
15	The moon at mid-autumn is especially bright	154
16	One can not become a doctor after taking medicine for three years	158

17	How much joy is travelling	162
18	There is no greater joy than making new friends	166
19	True beauty comes from within	169
20	The soaring melody halts the fleeting clouds	172
21	The flowers and trees I planted form a little path	176
22	Contentment is found when sought in serenity	179
23	Stealing half a day of bliss from the rush of life	183
24	The hair grows pale but the colour of one's native accent is unfading	186
25	A general's glory, ten thousand bodies	190
26	How should I find ten thousand manors	194
27	A stone that is fit for a wall is not left on the highway	198
28	Empty oneself of desires and nobility follows	201

About the Translators 205

1 Planning for the year ahead in spring

> *A person who has harboured great aspirations since young might not always succeed, but I dare say that those who were without any great dreams in their youth will simply be carried along by the current, drifting aimlessly, with no accomplishment to their names.*

"Plan for the year in the Spring, for the day in the morning, for a lifetime with diligence." This saying indicates the importance of laying a firm foundation during the early days of any endeavour, for only thus will you see your efforts flower; a weak foundation in a missed season merely paves the way for failure.

When Spring returns and all things on earth are rejuvenated in the first month of the lunar year, you should create a master plan for all you intend. Only ensure that the planning is rational, reasonable, and follow it through in the accepted and proper manner. At the end of the year, evaluate everything to ascertain how much of that year's plan has been realised. Should there be efforts that have not come to fruition, you should then reflect on the reasons for why things went amiss and seek the means to redeem the situation, these reflections anticipating and guiding your planning for the coming year.

As regards the day, it is the morning hours that are truly precious. After eight hours of sound sleep, a person's spirit is completely revived. The air is especially pure and fresh at this time. With the rising sun awakening the earth with its glorious rays, all who are greeted by this splendid glow will feel radiant. If you can devote 2 to 3 hours of total concentration to your work at this hour, you will find yourself more efficient than if you had slogged through 7 to 8 hours of work in the office during the course of the day. How true is the saying "Three early risings, one day gained". Recharged in the morning, you will be able to handle anything and everything that comes your way. Should you make good use of the early morning hours, engaging in your life's endeavors with wholehearted devotion, you will assuredly have a very bright future.

Youth is a person's golden age. When Chinese historians from ancient times wrote biographies of famous or successful persons, they usually began by saying that the person "had held great aspirations since young". A person who has had great aspirations since young might not always succeed, but I dare say that those who were without any great dreams in their youth would simply be carried along by the current, drifting aimlessly, with no accomplishment to their names. "Great aspiration" may be understood, more simply, as "having a noble ambition".

I often say that the secondary school years are the most important time of a person's life. During a child's primary school years, a child has limited ability to digest and absorb what is being learned; by the time the child enters university, the teacher is there merely to provide guidance. Such a teaching style benefits students with strong foundations, but is like "playing the *qin* before kine①" when dealing with weaker students; they will take down notes too slowly and find the required reading text and writing assignments an utterly insurmountable task. Even were such a student eventually scrape by with a diploma, that qualification would be valueless both to himself and others. It is thus only during the secondary school years, when the students' ability to digest and absorb knowledge is at its peak, that the teacher is able to nurture their values and personality, instil basic discipline in their studies, foster their interest and cultivate their study methods; the improvement is then noticeable on a daily and semestral basis. We need only to look at some of those honoured men who received only a secondary education but whose academic and meritorious achievements far outweigh those of the many holding graduate qualifications. From this, we might observe that those who lay a good foundation during their secondary school years are better equipped to choose how to advance as opportunities avail themselves.

In fact, in academic, planning is needed; in building a house, planning is needed; in governing a country still yet more imperative is the need for planning. The king of Yue, Gou Jian, devoted ten years to increasing the population and wealth of his kingdom, and another ten years to the education of his people. For this reason it might be said of him that he was the first statesman in history to have put in place a national plan for the economy and the people's livelihood. It is immeasurably wiser to have a plan to guide one's efforts as opposed to blindly groping in the dark without one; this applies throughout: from the individual to society, from country to entire world, and to all the myriad professions and occupations that exist.

We know the world to be imperfect, and that not every meaningful project comes to fruition; the project might end up withering even before it is ever implemented. Yet we firmly believe that had no plans existed, the situation in that case would have been utterly untenable. On that note, it should also be said that an accessible and sensible plan is more likely to succeed than a grandiose one.

To be honest, were I able to understand your aspirations or ambitions, I would be able to anticipate most of your actions, well before they have been brought to full articulation.

Written on March 27, 1955, late at night

Notes:

① playing the *qin* before kine: a useless effort to tell someone about something which they have no capacity to understand. An English idiomatic equivalent would be 'casting pearls before swine'. The *qin* is the Chinese zither.

2   Carrying dry rations when full, an umbrella on a clear day

> *Almost every person has the opportunity to pursue his ambition, but most people do a poor job of preparing for it, such that when the opportunity arises, they are unable to seize it. Winning and losing are an integral part of life's struggle. The final victory, therefore, belongs to those sufficiently prepared.*

In China's rural communities, families of moderate means usually hang couplets and paintings in the family hall. Of the various couplets and paintings, *Zhu Bolu's teachings about family affairs*[①] are widely popular among the rural folk. Zhu Bolu taught that: "It is advisable to repair the doors and windows before rain comes, but woe to those who dig their wells only when they are thirsty." I feel, however, that these wise sayings are neither as colloquial nor as vigorous as, "Carry dry rations when full, and an umbrella on a clear day".

The difference between an intelligent man and an average person lies in the former's ability to see further ahead than the latter, the former is therefore able to make his move first and in so doing, seizes the advantage. The average person cobbles together a plan in an ad-hoc fashion, and is not properly prepared for anything. When faced with setbacks and difficulties, he is left floundering and resentful of his situation. In fact, all things in this world are subject to the laws of causality. The expert is thus not necessarily greatly superior to the average person; instead he is one who pays particular attention to the laws of causality, capable of discerning how a sequence of events unfolds, the whys and wherefores, and thus has the upper hand and foresight in any given situation. Such foresight arms him with a readiness in the face of the unexpected and enables him to deal with any contingencies or crises with a focused, untroubled mind, resolving them with equanimity.

How knowledgeable a person is depends on the standard to which he has been trained, the kind of study and research methods he has been using, whether he has had the benefit of good teachers, and acquired good friends. Regular investment and effort in learning about a particular subject enables one to write rigorously, and also with depth. One not given to preparation, however, will have nothing to draw on when the need arises; no matter how hard one might rack one's brain, one will only be able, regretfully, to turn in a blank sheet.

Almost everyone is given the opportunity to pursue his ambitions, but most people make a poor job of preparing for it, such that when the opportunity arises, they are unable to seize it. The strategist creates opportunities; the average person at least grasps those that present themselves, but the nonchalant and unprepared can only watch as golden opportunities elude them, time and again.

Winning and losing are an integral part of life's struggles. The final victory, thus, belongs to those sufficiently prepared. The path towards success being never straightforward, one should expect obstacles and setbacks as part of the vicissitudes of life. Should your first line of defence be breached, you can fall back on your second line; when that fails, the third yet remains. To be able to soldier on despite defeat, be persistent and endure difficulties—that is what true heroism is made of. On the other hand, to be consistently ill-prepared causes one to succumb quickly to adversity as soon as it appears. In *Aesop's Fables* may be found the story of a wild boar and a fox. A wild boar was standing under a tree, sharpening its tusks against the tree bark. A passing fox asked the boar why it did this despite there being no apparent danger from either hunter or hound. It replied: "I considered carefully before I decided to do this, for I would not have the time to spare when I actually need my tusks in times of danger." Such vigilance in times of peace is precisely what is imperative in the struggle for survival.

A person who takes Beijing Opera seriously will rise early every morning to exercise his voice, regardless of whether he is to perform that day. One with a passion for martial arts will set aside time to train daily, no matter if he is to compete. And so, the adage goes "the hand is ever shaped to fist, the song forever in the mouth". A person not normally given to preparation will burn the midnight oil before the competition, by which time he will be so frantically exhausted that, even before the match, he already stands defeated.

Effort in preparation never goes to waste; instead, it saves much time and energy. To affirm the importance of preparedness, we should always be mindful of the saying "Carry dry rations when full, an umbrella on a clear day".

Written on 13th January, 1955, early morning

Notes:

① Zhu Bolu: A Neo-Confucianist from the early Qing Dynasty (1617−1688). His *Teachings about the family affairs*, also known as the *Zhuzi Instructions for the Family*, is widely popular.

3   It is all owed to the wellspring, its running water

> *If a person wants to get ahead in his studies, he must, since youth, have established a firm foundation; only then will his efforts bear fruit in future.*

The pond opens out, a half-*mu* of clear mirror,
As sky-light and cloud-shadow dance off its shimmering face.
Why, one asks, is the pond so clear?
It is owing to its wellspring, its running water.
　　　　　— (Song Dynasty) Zhu Xi, *Reflections upon reading*

This piece by Zhu Xi is no ordinary poem but the distillation of an enlightened mind. Of the affairs of the world, only the deeply rooted are inexhaustible; a shallow source depletes resources rapidly, leaving one flailing and floundering, helpless and pathetic.

"A depth of reading, a wealth of wisdom." My young friends, reading regularly enables the amassing of a wealth of knowledge, this accumulated wealth being the key to writing well. In particular, take frequent notes, and jot down all your thoughts, insights and any useful material. Then annotate and footnote the texts you have read and compile an index on your own. In this way, you will have all the relevant resources, summarised and clarified, laid out before you when you write. Having the necessary materials to hand, your writing will at least be generally substantial. Furthermore, careful attention to the works of famous writers, and being alert to how they lay out the structure and plot, their creative expressions and words play, will surely make you more aware of how these serve to render your writing more engaging and vivid. With more practice and refinement, your writing will become more substantial. When you are able to write with substance, coherence, precise understanding and linguistic expressiveness, you would have already tapped into the wellspring of running water within yourself. In this case, your inspiration will gush forth unbidden, unbridled. Whether writing an epic or a work of prose, you will enjoy the sense of empowerment and adequacy, having left the days of painful gestation far behind.

In modern English literature, none can claim the same achievements as George Bernard Shaw[1]. Thoroughly schooled in the knowledge of music since childhood, Shaw delved deeply into the works of Jonathan Swift[2]. Such ability alone justifies his high reputation as art critic and humorist. He specialised in the drama of Ibsen[3], then in vogue throughout Europe, while compiling his definitive volume *The Quintessence of Ibsenism*. With the vastness of his knowledge and his ability to distill the essence of things, masterworks spilled forth from Shaw's pen as he devised many of his problem plays.

Should a person desire to progress academically, a firm foundation for studies in his youth must be built before his efforts can bear fruit in the future. In other words, if one has not mastered the Chinese and English languages during one's secondary school years, the future will be fraught with frustration even though one might reach tertiary or post-tertiary levels. You might be able to learn from other branches of knowledge, but your ability to absorb and perform will surely be very limited. Similarly, the lack of a strong foundation in mathematics during your secondary school years will cause you to struggle if you want to specialise in mathematics, physics or chemistry. As for music, most educated families today begin their child's musical education when he is 5 or 6. These children would have become music experts by their 20s. If a child be allowed to waste his early years, when will the adult find the time to build that foundation? By then, he will be burdened by the responsibilities of earning a living, resolving personal disputes and facing the unrelenting chaos life throws at him, with hardly a moment of respite.

My young friends, if you realise the value of "the wellspring of running water", you should engage with all haste in studies that are grounded and which will take you far in the future, rather than gaining knowledge through hearsay, or blindly following the crowd. Only thus will you be able to think independently and be able to discern right from wrong, for these things are the *sine qua non* of every thinker, scholar and writer.

Written on May 1, 1955 on Labor Day

Notes:

① George Bernard Shaw (1856–1950): a famous British playwright and art critic.

② Jonathan Swift (1667–1745): British author, whose books include *Gulliver's Travels*.

③ Henrik Ibsen (1828–1906): famous Norwegian playwright, whose works include *A Doll's House*.

4 Making a name for yourself by becoming an expert in one area

> *In this day and age, we need to acquire a broad breadth of general knowledge while having an in-depth understanding in our area of specialisation. A true scholar or artist must elect to devote his lifetime to the pursuit of one or two areas of study, in accordance to his personality and environment.*

As the saying goes, a jack of all trades, is master of none. A person with a basic understanding of every type of skill, but without gaining proficiency in any, will end up desolate and impoverished, such that even surviving from day to day is a challenge.

All humans are differently gifted, some with very specialised gifts while others are talented in various ways. In theory, those with very focused areas of development are more likely to succeed in life; those with multiple specializations, however, might well also find success. However, one's time and energy are limited. When one is devoted to developing any single talent, it cannot help but be the case that his other talents will be neglected, for one cannot spin and reel at the same time.

In encyclopaedias or biographies, we frequently encounter this kind of opening description: Mr. or Miss so-and-so, something-ist. For example: Edward Gibbon, historian; Charles Dickens, novelist; John Maynard Keynes, economist ... the list continues. A scholar or an artist might possess several notable abilities, but history only records his most significant achievements while omitting the rest. In fact, were a person able to leave his mark on academic or artistic areas, or even in his career, it would earn him renown. Conversely, were he to attempt proficiency in everything he laid his hands on, he might end up with mediocre accomplishments, even failure. Before long, he would be forgotten by history.

When we talk about Chinese calligraphy, a particularly monumental figure looms large—the "Sage of Calligraphy"—Wang Xizhi. Wang Xizhi was a professional calligrapher. He started by absorbing the essence of the calligraphic styles of Han and Wei Dynasties Tablets, and mastered the styles to the extent that he could create his own unique style. The expression "iron strokes silver hooks" sums up his unique style most aptly. Having said that, we must remember that he was not a superhuman born with inherent skills, but an ordinary person who learned through struggle. It was only because he had mastered the skill of calligraphy (through the Eight Methods of the character 永) and through his hard work "by the pond[①]", that he was able to concentrate in his work and write with a brush so fully under his control, that it seemed divinely sanctioned. While noted in the history of Chinese literature as an epistolarian, his greatest achievement lies in calligraphy, the art which he poured his life and soul into mastering.

Last year, when viewing the engravings of the miniaturist sculptor② Huang Laofen, I marvelled at the fineness of his strokes, the clarity of his handwriting, the neatness of the rows of characters, all of which were meticulously executed. As I watched him carve away, I noted the intense concentration, tightly controlled breathing and his hands that barely moved. When he had finished, the engravings could hardly be made out with the naked eye. It was only through inspecting his handiwork under a magnifying glass that one could fully appreciate the intricacy of his work. While this might seem a trivial skill, he had to invest at least one or two decades of hard work before giving a public exhibition.

The fact is, when a person is willing to pursue an academic or artistic specialisation relentlessly, achieving success is only a matter of time.

In this technologically-advanced age, our job scope is increasingly finely divided and delegated. A person must be proficient in a specific skill before he can make a living and settle down. Barring a few special people who do not fall under the restrictions of the system, ordinary high school graduates must endure five to seven years of specialised training before they can become doctors, lawyers, accountants, engineers or musicians. Where literature, history, philosophy and the natural sciences are concerned, the time required to delve deeply in studies is virtually endless. Those who have received their degrees can at most be said to have found the right path. As to becoming more proficient in fields of research and invention, it would require unremittingly hard work from then on.

We need, in this day and age, to have a broad breadth of general knowledge while also having an in-depth knowledge in our area of specialisation. A true scholar or artist must elect to devote his or her lifetime to pursuing one or two areas of study, in accordance to his personality and environment. One should humble oneself to learn from others, while continuing to strive hard. The motto for the start of every new day should be "renew, refresh, revivify". Three days of non-study will dull one's mind. For this reason, one must not cease to plough on. In fact, should you devote yourself to proper research, you will eventually achieve mastery through having comprehensively studied the subject.

Written on April 3, 1955 late at night

Notes:

① by the pond: According to legend, the Han Dynasty calligrapher Zhang Zhi practiced calligraphy next to a pond, in which he washed his ink-stone, doing this so diligently that the pool of water turned black. From then on, the act of practising calligraphy has sometimes been known in Chinese as "by the pond".

② miniaturist sculptor: artist who engraves characters or sculptures on tiny surfaces, such as a strand of hair or rice grains.

5 Who can still study when he is old [1]

> *When a person enters upon middle-age or old-age, he is not as energetic as he was when young, and he is heavily burdened with having to maintain his family and deal with the complications and disputes with people. In short, he simply will not have a moment's peace. Wearied and idle, he can hardly be bothered even to read the newspapers, let alone a book.*

Youth is truly one's golden age. For the young person, reading for the purposes of learning is simple, and he can also easily play to his heart's content. Simply put, regardless of profession, it is not difficult for a young person to stand out and be proficient in it.

While we agree with the idea of "late bloomers", the word "late" in this expression refers to a longer grooming period than is the norm, and to achieving success later in one's life. This, however, does not mean that a person should set aside their books in their youth, and behave like the foolish man who waits for a rabbit by a tree②, expecting the "late blooming" to happen by itself. I admit that knowledge from books is only part of learning, but it is undoubtedly the most important aspect. As books record the experiences of distinguished people from China and other countries, from past to present, the reader can adopt these experiences as his foundation, or at least serve as a reference point, to be augmented by his own experiences. Only then will he attain great achievement. To ignore those records would be effectively to close one's eyes to the experiences of these predecessors and prominent historical persons, as one attempts to reinvent the wheel single-handedly. If this were the way of things, civilisation would never progress.

There is no limit to learning, and as long as one lives, one learns; and even as one learns till he is old, there will always be things yet to be learned. However, where learning is concerned, the young are better off at grasping lessons than the middle-aged, while the middle-aged outstrip the old. As the ancients lamented, "Had I worked harder when young and vigorous, I should not have vain regrets now that I am old and frail".

Everyone knows how abundantly energetic the young are. Most importantly, they do not need to worry about the running of a household and are therefore able to commit themselves to their studies fully. On the other hand, most people would display the signs of ageing with "sight failing, hair silvering, and teeth wobbling③" as early as at the age of 40, perhaps due to inherent weaknesses that are compounded with the natural wear and tear of the ageing process.

While the young remain unwearied even when working at something all day long, the average middle-aged person is exhausted after just three or four hours of effort. This decline in energy will transform one's outlook on life from a resplendent marigold to a dull, murky grey.

Just when one's energy declines as one ages, one is at the same time burdened with that most troubling concern of earning a living. Many people do not get to apply what they learned, instead having to work at something they are unschooled in. Indeed, it is not easy to find a suitable job that allows you to demonstrate your unique talents. Even if you found a compatible job, you would still have to cope with many unexpected conflicts and disputes.

You see, when a person enters middle or old-age, he is not as energetic as he was when young, and he is heavily burdened with maintaining his family as well as by the complications and disputes with people. In short, he simply will not have a moment's peace. Wearied and idle, he will hardly be bothered to even read the newspapers, let alone a book.

In ancient times, monks were considered the most learned among the Chinese people. Monks had no problems with providing for their own simple needs; if we consider their philosophy of "coming and going unencumbered", they are relatively free from the complications and disputes with people.

They answer the call of the morning bell, rising before the sun and devoting themselves to chanting the sutra. With only a handful of important Buddhist scriptures to recite, even a monk of moderate intelligence will be able to derive some enlightenment after reciting, memorizing and meditating on these scriptures again and again for decades on end. This proves that the "old" may yet be able to study and engage in scholarly pursuits. However, such opportunities are scarce. For the majority, learning opportunities will be sharply limited upon leaving school. Unless they have developed healthy reading habits since young and cultivated their aptitude of learning, such that they treasure every stolen moment amidst their busy lives, fully maximising these learning moments, I am afraid it is very difficult for these people to make progress.

"Who can still study when he is old?" This expression is not meant to discourage the middle-aged, but rather to warn the young to lay a sound foundation while they yet possess boundless energy, carefree lives and unperturbed minds. How their future will bear fruit will depend wholly upon the depth of their foundations.

Written on October 2, 1955 at the Harbour View Hotel

Notes:

① The title "Who can still study when old?" is taken from a poem by the Tang Dynasty poet Wang Jin (i.e. Wang Wei's younger brother), which goes "If one does not make a name for himself within the first two decades of life, who can still study when he is old? Then, alone in the forest, he can only drink wine borrowed from his neighbour, and listen to the occasional sounds of a passing elder's chariot."

② The Chinese proverb tells of a foolish man waiting by a tree for a rabbit to come along and dash its head against the tree. It demonstrates the futility of a lazy person who relies on chance to provide for him.

③ From the poet Han Yu's "Eulogy to Shi-er Lang".

6 The mansion is windswept as a mountain storm approaches

> *I would advise everyone to learn more about history. In addition to a country's history, people in various trades should also understand the history of their trades. Only then will they have insight into the past, understand the present and grasp the future.*

A person who understands the law of causality will have a clear grasp of the relationship between the causes and effects of events. He understands that nothing ever happens *ex nihilo*, and that there must be reasons why something occurs; once he is able to pinpoint the reasons for it, he can predict with reasonable accuracy how events will eventually evolve and conclude.

Sages from ancient China took the law of causality very seriously. They would derive a body of philosophy regarding the law before applying it to matters concerning men, and were especially reflective in areas involving warfare, politics and economics. Were I to use two phrases to summarise their theories, these would be, first, "to discern the direction of the wind by observing how the blade of the grass moves" and, second, "to adapt according to one's circumstances so as to exploit fully the advantages presented". The first phrase emphasises the study of causality, while the latter applies the understanding of the principles. Both, if applied suitably, will facilitate the smooth flowing of things in accordance with one's desire, and enable one to grasp the relations of the whole from its parts.

Before the advent of rain, ants would have already started scurrying, moving their colony to higher ground. The tiny ants are without the benefit of meteorological services, nor are they equipped with sophisticated instruments. They rely instead on experience, from knowing that when air pressure is too low, the underground becomes damp, and movement impeded; they must immediately move the colony from the wetter lowland to the dry high terrain. Only thus may they avoid drowning. The young ants observe their elders' actions, find them sensible, and thus unconsciously mimic them. And so, when the weather is about to change, they will also move the colony ahead of the rain.

Those who have studied economics will surely know what a "business cycle" is. When commerce prospers, most businesses will be profitable. When the general sentiment is optimistic, banks are more generous with dispensing loans. Unfortunately, in a free market economy, everything is unregulated and unplanned. Sometimes, when a business sector is over-invested, causing overproduction that results in oversupply, the market will stagnate, with sales plummeting and inventories piling up. Business owners will long for a quick sale so as to clear their stockpile by whatever means. Seeing things taking an unfavourable turn, banks adopt a tightening policy to demand repayment from these struggling factories and businesses. Caught between sluggish sales for their goods and pressure from banks to honour their liabilities, factories and businesses face liquidity problems. As a result, some factories and businesses will have to close down, and some of those who are held accountable for such loss might even commit suicide out of desperation. As a result, the market descends into chaos, businesses fail, and the economy plunges into deep depression.

During a market downturn, some more fortunate businesses with strong financial backing may escape the worst of the storm with some clever manoeuvring. After suffering a loss, they will have learned a lesson. And as the saying goes: survive a catastrophe and good fortune follows. They will be more prudent than before, taking sure steps in all their ventures, developing new markets, reducing expenditure while opening up new sources of revenue, and also keeping a healthy balance sheet. Companies reinforce their credibility by consistently breaking even or running a surplus. When the opportunity arises, they will again be able to tap on funds from the bank whereby to expand their businesses. With the right strategies, the market may be rejuvenated and start to turn in handsome profits in less than a year.

In short, the intelligent are set apart from the ordinary by virtue of being able to "discern the direction of the wind by observing how the blade of the grass moves" and gain from it a foreknowledge of all things. Ordinary people are mostly enlightened on hindsight; only when the rain has passed and the sky cleared do they awaken to realise that they have encountered a storm. To remedy this deficiency, I would advise everyone to learn more about history. In addition to a country's history, people in various trades should also understand the history of their own trades. Only then will they have insight into the past, understand the present and grasp the future. Since our current situation is a result of the past's myriad causes, the diligence and wisdom we invest in today will also be causes that determine the shape of our future. We reap what we sow; this, in a nutshell, is what causality is all about.

"The mansion is wind-swept as a mountain storm approaches." This expression illustrates the fact that what is currently observed is also an index to what lies ahead. If a person does not read history nor observe all the signs of the moment, and only knows to work against the course of nature with only his own counsel for a guide, then his future is probably worse off than that of even the most humble of ants.

Written April 24, 1955

7 The waves of the Yangtze River surge ever forward

> *Learning is a never-ending quest, and the word "complacency" certainly has no place in the process. Conversely, it is the realisation upon finishing a course of learning that there is still much more to learn that causes one to strive to deepen one's learning in order to compensate for what remains deficient.*

"The waves of the Yangtze River surge ever forward; the new generation replaces the old."

The years march on relentlessly, fading away into oblivion as the days go by. Regardless of your progress, time rolls on like the waves of the Yangtze, departing resolutely into the east, day and night. Take a man of 45, who has accomplished little in life, and compare him with a strapping young man, full of verve and unencumbered by family responsibilities. Within a few years of hard work, the young man will have overtaken the older man. Whether he likes it or not, the older man will be left behind by the wayside.

To avoid becoming redundant, we must avoid complacency, for time moves ever forward. Yesterday's sensational news is today's old news; in two days' time, it is already obsolete. Emperor Tang of the Shang Dynasty was an outstanding head of state whose motto was: "When possible, throw out the old and continually renew yourself, never-ceasing, ever-vivifying.[①]" Indeed, in this era of rapid scientific progress, a person who is self-indulgent or complacent effectively commits suicide. Learning is a never-ending quest, and the word "complacency" certainly has no place in the process. Conversely, it is the realisation upon finishing a course of learning that there is still much more to learn that causes one to strive to deepen one's learning in order to compensate for what remains deficient. Build up your treasury of knowledge, live out what you learn, for all these will come together for you in the fullness of time.

Man's greatest failing is his inability to know himself. While anyone would agree that it is not right to be complacent, no one is fully aware of whether he might already be trapped in the state of complacency. At the same time, there may be no one willing to point this out to him. On the one hand, with accumulated age, one starts to flaunt one's seniority and the people around adopt a "keep him at arm's length" attitude; on the other hand, that individual might have achieved some "status" within the community and hold some real power. As a result, his worldly-wise subordinates will simply concur with all he says, for who will be willing to speak the truth to his face?

In the journey of life, all travellers are like cars in a long-distance race. Every racing car appears to be evenly matched as they form up at the starting point; but midway, some cars develop mechanical failure, and some drivers lose control of their cars, crashing out of the race. In this racing competition, no participant slows down or stops for you to finish your repair before continuing with you, hand in hand. On the contrary, when your car is in trouble, it is held to be your misfortune or your own inexcusable fault. For on the racing field, there is no room for chivalry or courtesy, and thus you only have yourself to blame for your misfortune or mistake; nobody will bear the punishment for you, nor offer you sympathy. After all, failure is failure, as, according to the age-old adage, "A defeated general speaks not of courage"; what more can you say?

Indeed, Confucius had foresight when he said: "The younger generation is formidable, so how can you know if those coming after you are not better than you? If you have yet to make a name for yourself by the time you are in your 40s or 50s, then you are no force to be reckoned with." This is especially the case with regard to the process of scientific research. All the new knowledge and new experiences that these "greenhorns" learn are probably far beyond the imagination of students from three or four decades ago. If the middle-aged think that they have made a name for themselves and are unwilling to continue to learn, then their careers are already doomed. According to a famous Chinese saying: one should "Judge a man only at his grave"; I believe, however, that a person who has neither the desire to improve nor aspiration may be considered "judged and condemned" even before he goes to his grave.

To avoid becoming obsolete with time, a person must keep on learning, seeking mentorship in all quarters. When you reach a stage where you are learning every day, then the younger ones will be so preoccupied with their admiration for you that they would have no reason to despise you. Conversely, those who have no desire to improve will only regress, for there is no middle ground for you wherein you might take a breather. You see, with wave after wave surging forward relentlessly, where could there ever be room for courtesy or chivalry?

Notes:

① This means "If it is possible to replace the old with the new, then we should do so, keeping ourselves constantly updated".

② The idiom originates from "The Book of Han". It means to be self-satisfied with old practices, with no desire for progress.

8 Disputes come from talking too much

In conversation, stay as much as possible on topics of consequence, and avoid judging the merits or ills of others.

"Diseases enter through the mouth; but from loose lips trouble slips." Gluttony and gossiping are the common failings of mankind, and unrelieved physical illnesses and personal disputes their unsavory fruits.

The ancient sages were always aware that words might easily go astray, and thus they repeatedly advised against talking too much. Lao tzu's observation to the effect that "The wise speak little, the fool babbles" has a great deal of sense in it. The wise know that action speaks louder than words, and that not lengthy speeches but concrete achievements are the best proof of one's worth. Conversely, it would be unwise to go around boasting without concrete achievements to back one up. Confucius adopted an even more cautious attitude towards speech. He was opposed to "clever words and flattering postures" and upheld instead "strength of character, simplicity in speech [1]". He was opposed to "subjugating people with eloquence", instead advocating "industrious work and cautious speech". In fact, the truly wise one does more and speaks less, while the average person chatters as much as he works. Only the basest individual brags incessantly, talks about himself in a way that is inconsistent with how he behaves, and speaks irresponsibly while caught up in the thrill of the moment. Fortunately, most people do not heed the words of such people who end by deceiving themselves and consequently losing all credibility and reputation.

Human beings are born with two ears and a mouth. This clearly suggests we should listen more to other people's opinions and give less voice to our own. In reality, however, the reverse is true. Whenever friends gather for conversation, no one can resist the chance to speak. In meetings, participants glory in fighting over the right to speak. Everyone wishes everyone else to "listen to what I have to say", but has no interest in hearing others out. This is the supreme irony.

If you have anything that you are delighted with, treasure that joy in your heart; refrain from expressing your happiness blatantly and from bragging about it. Those with more savoir-faire should just reply "I got lucky" with a smile when others congratulate them, and not strut about basking in others' praises. Decline the praise of others, and combat self-importance yet more vigorously. Do not indulge in your successes especially in front of those who are down, for that will cause the listener to be self-conscious of his own inadequacy and feel uncomfortable. Anyone so insensitive to others truly deserves whatever ill befalls them!

We tend to commit two mistakes in the normal course of conversation: criticising another's shortcomings and exaggerating our own strengths. Our fingers are naturally of different lengths, and so are people born with strengths and weaknesses; many people nonetheless enjoy gossiping about others, recalling only their shortcomings and exaggerating these for comic effect. The jester may enjoy his moment of fun, but once the butt of the joke comes to hear of it, resentment will inevitably build. "Self-defence" is a human instinct, and everyone knows to mask his own weaknesses from others. Should a person's weakness be inadvertently uncovered by others and made the talk of the town, it will naturally infuriate him.

Whenever friends gather, everyone should be given the chance to speak. Should a newcomer be present, the host should try to engage him in conversation, so as to avoid leaving the guest out and spoiling the party. In conversation, stay as much as possible on topics of consequence, and avoid judging the merits or ills of others. Even when passing comment on a living individual, keep to the spirit of "avoiding the faults, and extolling the merits," spending more effort on praising another's strength and less on criticizing their weaknesses. Encourage, not criticise; be sympathetic rather than combative: this will serve to strengthen a friendship.

This is not to say that one ought to be an opinionless "Mr. Nice Guy". What I am trying to say is: as far as possible, we should have some consideration for another's feelings. For while praise might not affect some, disparagement may inflict deep injury. "Hurtful words are hard to stomach", and thus, in this, we should remain vigilant.

Written on February 19, 1955 early morning

Notes:

① Strength of character, simplicity in speech. Confucius says that anyone who possesses these virtues comes close to embodying integrity of spirit and benevolence of heart.

9   Enmity should be resolved, not engendered

> *Forgiveness is a virtue that philosophers all over the world extol. Rather than allow yourself to be small-minded, why not be magnanimous and forgive?*

Generally speaking, enmity is usually born out of these things: competing for fame, fortune, power, sex. These things are the main causes of rancor and hatred. From the examination hall, some emerge victorious, others vanquished. When there is a great disparity in competence between the parties involved, nothing much occurs; it is when both parties are evenly matched that problems ensue. Where the stakes are particularly high, the loser inevitably resorts to schemes and machinations so as to bring down the victor, with the victimized party bitterly desiring retaliation. An eye for an eye, a tooth for a tooth—thus does enmity descend into a vicious cycle of destruction.

Fame has always been contended over in imperial courts, and profits, in the marketplace. In literary or political circles, ranking is the prize; in the business world, wealth is the measure of success. While you want to make money, others also wish to prosper; wealth is finite but greed unbounded. When the winds of recession course through the market, when people struggle to make ends meet, they start to panic. Consequently, they resort to trickery, counterfeiting trademarks, engaging in fraud, bribery and smuggling. Should these schemes fail, the consequences are simple and fairly straightforward; however, when they do succeed, the aggrieved victim will most certainly nurse a grudge.

The average person is mostly concerned with making a fortune, while more sophisticated people seek fame, following which they quest after power. This ambition drove Julius Caesar[①] to conquer the whole of Europe, and was also the cause of his violent death at the hands of assassins. As for the character Feng Jie from the Chinese classic *The Dream of the Red Chamber*, she was not content to luxuriate in the opulence of the Da Guan Mansion[②] but kept seeking opportunities to lord over others through her overseeing of events and the exercise of domestic discipline and intrigue, her actions proclaiming her to be someone craving domination. A person in power naturally inspires awe; the powerless, on the other hand, inevitably resort to chicanery. History and stories abound with people who behaved like this, of these I see no point in making a list.

In the old days, marriages were usually arranged by parents, so there are fewer stories of ugly fights over romantic affairs; on the other hand, such fights happened more frequently in seedier places that involved jealous patrons fighting among themselves for the favour of popular courtesans.

To form deep enmity with another in the name of fame, fortune, power or sex is already a grave mistake; should one decide to take it further by vengeful retaliation, it would be even more lamentable. Revenge is nothing but an exercise in futility.

Ordinary people with some power or authority seek revenge by hauling their opponents before the court over trivial matters, demanding that the other party apologise or pay compensation for the damage to their "honour". By seeking revenge for every wrong and injustice, they display a pathetic lack of humor.

Confucius counsels: "Do not offer to explain that which has transpired, do not try to convince otherwise of what has been done, do not call to account for what has already passed." Forgiveness is a virtue that philosophers all over the world extol. Rather than allow yourself to be small-minded, why not be magnanimous and forgive? We should consider, carefully, whether the injury is dealt consciously or unintentionally. If it has been dealt out of malice, then it is a different matter altogether; but if unintentional, it should be forgiven. After all, human beings are creatures of emotion. If the other party sees that you do not bear a grudge, he will certainly be grateful; he might perhaps even turn over a new leaf and become righteous for the rest of his life.

As for those with malign intent, rather than expending time and effort in out-maneuvering them, it is better to mobilize the power of society to subdue them. As the saying goes, "he who does great evil digs his own grave." Although the deceit of the evil-doer may, through sheer luck, succeed in the short term, he will eventually pay the price for their deeds, of this we are absolutely certain.

Just as an individual ought to avoid making enemies, so too should nations. Some countries look for enemies everywhere while relentlessly developing weapons in order to achieve their goals. They are ignorant of the fact that their efforts are futile when viewed from a broader perspective, for the outcome of a war is never certain; besides, while the defeated suffers from his loss, the victor, too, pays a price.

Indeed, enmity should be resolved, not engendered. Such a way of thinking not only prevents many unnecessary disputes, but is also the grand means to achieve world peace. Why don't we strive to follow the right path, instead of calling down trouble upon ourselves?

Written on March 6, 1955 at dawn

Notes:

① Gaius Julius Caesar (102 B. C.—44 B. C.): ancient Roman statesman and military strategist active in the political arena.

② Wang Xifeng was part of the Rong-guo household, not one of the denizens of the Da Guan Yuan. (Ed.)

10   A moment of misstep, an eternity of regret

> *Since we know that cowardice, carelessness, indiscretion, and weak will are the roots of much evil, we should work at cultivating judiciousness, being at once bold and thorough, while exercising self-restraint and strengthening our will power.*

Success and failure are not a plank's space apart; sometimes that which separates the two might be tissue-thin. Ancient sayings such as "Great treachery passes off as faithfulness, great wisdom as foolishness" illustrate the point that while treachery and faithfulness, wisdom and foolishness are, on the surface, absolute dichotomous pairs. In real life, they may scarcely be differentiable from each other. There is an old saying in China "To miss by a hair is to miss by a thousand miles".

Before a person acts, he must have a "motive" or "intent". Pure motives and good intentions bring results that are beneficial to others and oneself; conversely, unwholesome intentions will, of necessity, be demonstrated by deeds harmful to others and oneself. The saying "you reap what you sow" essentially demonstrates the law of causality at work, and the outcome is something we humans can do nothing to affect.

In general, a person's failure can be equally attributed to the environment and personality. Although some people displace all blame onto their environment, or all responsibility onto the individual, this is a biased perspective that is not fit to serve as a model of conduct.

A person must be bold when he is starting up a new venture, and boldness entailing both courage and shrewdness. In embarking on a new business, success is never guaranteed. A timid person who fears ridicule or failure will end up surrendering even before trying, and is doomed right from the start.

If cowardice and carelessness are the main causes of one's failure, indiscretion also leads to self-defeat. Indiscreet people tend to be frivolous, speaking at the wrong time and place, and to the wrong audience, just so as to be heard. Chapter 72 of the Chinese classic *Romance of Three Kingdoms* records the story of the death of the character Yang Xiu. In the story, Yang Xiu deciphered the meaning behind the marching order issued by Chancellor Cao Cao, "Chicken ribs[①]", and packed up his belongings without permission in preparation for a withdrawal. When Cao Cao added the character "live" (活) in his calligraphy of the character "door[②]" (门), Yang Xiu interpreted the gesture as the Chancellor's complaining that the garden door was too wide, and so took the initiative to build up the wall to make the door narrower. In another incident, Cao Cao wrote the words "one box of biscuits" (一合酥) which Yang Xiu interpreted to mean "one mouthful of biscuits for everyone[③]" (一人一口酥), and so shared out the biscuits without seeking the permission of the owner. On yet another occasion, Cao Cao devised a scheme to kill his opponents by faking a dream, but Yang Xiu exposed it by saying that, "The Chancellor is not dreaming; it is you, dear sir, who are still dreaming." Though Yang Xiu discerned correctly in each of these instances, he was speaking out of turn;, what he said was extremely inappropriate. Unfortunately, Yang Xiu was indiscreet in being too eager to display his talents, and was executed for "sowing unrest among the troops". This story illustrates the consequences of being indiscreet and attention-seeking, these ranging from humiliation to losing one's life.

I should also like to point out that a weak will is the driving force behind all evil and all degenerate behaviour. I have a friend who was a primary school principal. On a chance occasion, he toured a casino. At first he did not even dare to look, but eventually curiosity got the better of him and he joined the crowd beside a gambling table as a bystander. While the gamblers used money to exchange for tokens, he was placing bets in his heart, and by some fluke of fortune, he managed to call all his bets correctly. Faced with the golden gleam of money, reason gave way to emotion and he tried his hand for the first time. At first he was still standing by the side, topping up others' bets with his own tokens. When he lost half the cash he had with him, an impulse made him discard his status as an honorable educator and sit down at the table, rolling up his sleeves and throwing himself wholly into the game. First went his cash, then his watch, then his wedding ring. Eventually, he returned to his hostel, drained and debt-ridden. The next day, news of his spree reached the Board of Directors, who convened an emergency meeting to sack the principal whose moral credibility as an educator and role model had been lost. After suffering this double blow, my friend was at his wits' end, and soon after he disappeared. When I next heard of him, he was dead. I could not help but lament "A moment of misstep, an eternity of regret!"

Indeed, the distinction between success and failure is wafer-thin. All it takes is a single moment of folly, and success becomes as remote as the stars. Since we know that cowardice, carelessness, indiscretion, and weak will are the roots of much evil, we should work at cultivating judiciousness, being at once bold and thorough, while exercising self-restraint and strengthening our will power. Bear in mind that it takes three years to learn virtue, but only three days to go astray. Decades of hard work may be utterly destroyed in a moment.

"A moment of misstep, an eternity of regret." When you fail, no amount of tears or regret will change a thing.

Written on March 20, 1955 early morning

Notes:

① Chicken ribs: a Chinese expression that means something that is useless yet a pity to discard.

② The Chinese character for the word "wide" (阔) is made up of the radical "door" (门) and the character "live" (活).

③ The Chinese character for "box" (盒) may sometimes be written as 合, which is composed of the radicals "person" (人), "one" (一) and "mouth(ful)"(口).

11   Flowers not yet fully to blossom, the moon not yet full

Flowers in full bloom will soon wither; the full moon eventually wane. Instead of lamenting over the wind-scattered, wilted flowers or the darkness of the waning crescent, why not marvel at the fragrant allure of a flower on the cusp of blooming or the ethereal elegance of the waxing moon. While the former signifies the regrets of an exhausted happiness, the latter is a promise of the boundless hope ahead.

Were I to use China as a representation of oriental culture, I dare say the spirit of traditional Chinese culture might be encapsulated in the following lines of a poem: "Flowers yet fully to blossom, the moon not yet full."

The mundane and the worldly might wish that flowers would remain always glorious and the moon always full; only thinkers with superior insight are able to appreciate the subtle beauty of "Flowers yet fully to blossom, the moon not yet full". This is not an ordinary poem; rather, it emblematises the Chinese philosopher's attitude towards life.

It is not that philosophers are unable to enjoy the pleasures of flowers in full bloom or a moon round and full. But flowers in full bloom will soon wither; the full moon must eventually wane. Instead of lamenting over the wind-scattered, wilted flowers or the darkness of the waning crescent, why not marvel at the fragrant allure of a flower on the cusp of blooming or the ethereal elegance of the waxing moon. While the former signifies the regrets of an exhausted happiness, the latter is a promise of the boundless hope ahead.

The Chinese are most particular about subtlety. In literature, we place great emphasis on the unspoken shades and tones of meaning in a piece of work. In landscaping, we enjoy the "winding pathways that lead to secret havens, shrubberies and woods that conceal the meditation chamber". Secrecy and concealment are the key to subtlety; if everything is laid bare and taken in at one glance, there will be nothing for one to savour.

The Chinese rarely resort to litigation, because whatever the outcome, there is some damage: the defeated of course loses the case, but winning the case deepens the grudge between the parties involved. Confucius once said that his ability to engage in a lawsuit was not inferior to the next person's, but he desired always to avoid bringing matters before the court. In fact, not only do the Chinese dislike lawsuits, they also extol the ultimate virtue of "parting ways without uttering words of malice". Otherwise, even if you manage to overwhelm the other party decisively on this occasion, how will you be able to face each other when next you meet?

In all things, know your limits and learn not to overdo, for this is the most sensible course to take. If you seek to pursue everything to the bitter end—and, in truth, there is no end—you merely invite further trouble. Whenever I see people everywhere smugly pronouncing that they intend to pursue someone relentlessly, I cannot help but wish to recite the wonderful couplet "flowers yet to fully bloom, the moon not yet full".

My frequent observations of the tide, moon and flowers have led me to some insight about life's vicissitudes. The best moment at which to admire the tide is when it has risen to 70 to 80 percent of its highest level, when the waves are rolling in mightily, and your heart soars in sympathetic exhilaration. When the tide reaches its highest point, the waves crash far up the beach and onlookers will have to retreat further inland to avoid getting wet, for that would really dampen the spirit and spoil the fun.

The ebbing tide leaves decomposing animal carcasses left along the beach, raising an unbearable stench. Thus, my preferred way of admiring the tides at the seaside would often be at the moment when the tide is rising but has yet to reach its peak, for the gradually rising tide will carry with it gusts of invigorating sea breeze.

The experiences of our predecessors and my personal observations on the matter has led me to concur deeply with the maxim "loosen your grip, expand your view". Close friends know that I refrain from wrangling with people, for that is a waste of precious energy. I may win for the moment and profit a little, but when there comes a pay-back time, the price will be unbearable.

As I strictly adhere to the doctrine of "flowers yet fully to blossom, the moon not yet full", I respect great people who are humble, calm and collected, and indifferent to fame and fortune. Gandhi and Tagore are two such people, as are Shaw and Rousseau; the person I admire most as my teacher is the Chinese poet Tao Yuanming, who was a man of modest desires.

"Drink but be not drunk; for there is more pleasure in mild inebriation." This should be the attitude of a person who knows how fully to enjoy the delights of "Flowers yet to fully to blossom, the moon not yet full".

Written on July 12, 1959 early morning

12 Fame will not crown the lazy head

Ingenuity leaves no mark, but hard work can be traced. You need constantly to strive on to become famous, but striving alone is no guarantee of fame. You see, what benefit can indolence bring you if even hard work might bring no fame?

Let me begin with a disclaimer: worldly fame—whether from achieving the top scholarly honours or from being rich and powerful—is not my theme. The fame I refer to is that of attaining the highest literary or artistic achievement. Even though such merit is cultivated in part by one's social and cultural background, it is still mostly dependent on one's real talent and learning.

Benjamin Franklin teaches us that "Diligence overcomes difficulties. Sloth makes them." This lesson is indeed true. Frankly speaking, a person who puts in real effort may be successful in some ways, but those who do not work hard will never succeed. This fact is crystal-clear. Wise mentors may, at most, point us to new methods or correct certain mistakes, but are of not much help to us in actually attaining artistic achievement. As Mencius said, "The craftsman may impart methods and standards to others, but not craftsmanship itself." These are the words of experience that Mencius distilled from his own hard work.

Time is relentless. Once gone, it never returns. Chinese poets lamented that "Time waits for no man", hence the English proverb "Time and tide wait for no man". For life is the accumulation of time. You only need to take a look at how you spend your days to ascertain if your life be meaningfully led. Should you squander your days in vain pursuits, then your life is indeed wasted. Time flows like running water, races on like a white stallion; in a blink of an eye it has sped through eight or ten years. It is not till you find yourselves becoming increasingly exhausted that you bemoan impotently "I have studied since young, but I am still far from being accomplished".

A person who has great achievements does not necessarily outlive the average person; it is just that the former maximises his time. Consider Su Dongpo and Leonardo da Vinci, the former a talented Chinese poet-scholar, the latter a knowledgeable, versatile European artist. Both lived only till they were middle-aged. Although both were born geniuses, blessed with a good learning environment, what stood out most about them was their phenomenal industry. Su recited *The Poetic Essay to the Epang Palace* till late at night all by himself, while Da Vinci kept sketchbooks and notes for as long as 40 years. These constituted their real capital, and their accomplishments in literature and the arts were only an exercise of that great capital.

Hard work demands nothing more than focus and perseverance. Staying focused can also be defined as "concentration of mind" or "single-mindedness". In reality, not only does the work of the professionals require them to be single-minded, the same is true of talented and learned persons. "There is always a pinnacle among the many peaks and valleys." The learned person may know many things, but all his knowledge and tools merely serve to help him achieve his ultimate goal. Only when we understand this can we appreciate the benefits of staying focused.

It is, however, not enough merely to stay focused, for we also need perseverance. In general, this is also the hardest discipline. Many people can labour away for day and night on end on impulse, but once they get over that phase, they sag, so disheartened and tired, that their original plans are totally abandoned and never to be revisited. In this case, the individual has become fickle-minded, which renders all his previous efforts utterly wasted.

Ingenuity leaves no mark, but hard work can be traced. You need constantly to strive on to become famous, but striving alone is no guarantee of fame. You see, what benefit can indolence bring you if even hard work might bring no fame?

Once you understand this, the expression "Fame crowns not the lazy head" becomes self-explanatory.

Written on February 12, 1955, late at night

13 The grass is always greener on the other side

We should bear in mind that it is wrong to whinge about one's job as one is doing it. The success in any job comes from much effort and energy. You can get on the path to success only if you are willing to think, work hard and find real joy in your work.

The human being is indeed a strange creature. He always complains about his job, whatever it may be. No matter what he does, he always feels that he has been short-changed while others have taken all kinds of advantage.

Sages of old have long perceived this common failing in humans of seeing the mote in the eye of others but not the log in their own. Mencius warned: "The eyes can see the tip of a fine hair but miss a cartful of wood." One may spot a tiny strand of hair when finding fault with others but miss seeing a cartful of wood when it comes to one's own fault. Isn't it strange that there should be such a discrepancy between one's view of others and oneself?

Were we to be harsh about it, people who whinge about their job are mostly good for nothing. The only key to becoming outstanding is to hold fast to one's own task. Such people will first carry out their duties, giving no thought to temporary gains or losses. They do not resort to trickery, speculation or say anything that goes against their beliefs because they understand that this can only deceive their readers or audience for a while but will eventually be seen through. Only those who hold firm to their post with integrity will succeed in winning the trust of their readers and audience over time.

I admire men in history who died defending the truth as they saw it, such as Qu Yuan, Wen Tianxiang, Shi Kefa, Socrates, Jesus, Galileo and Gandhi. Did they not love life? Yet, when they saw injustice at work, they would rather sacrifice themselves and die for what they saw as a just cause. To them, reputation, their career and academic essays were, variously, the most valuable things in this world, treasures for which they would unreservedly reject any offer in exchange. You see, if these men could even scorn life and wealth in the name of their life's work, would they whinge about what they do?

Confucius said: "Should a person hear the truth in the day, even if he were to pass away in the evening, it is arguable that he will die contented to know that he has not idled his life away." This philosophy helped Confucius cultivate a resolve that never tired of learning, nor impatient of teaching despite starvation and cold, this spirit earning him the just accolade as the "Teacher of All Ages". In the same way, Jesus taught, "You should acknowledge your saviour openly." These words have a special meaning to young people who devote their lives to society. Their dedication means that they cannot back out or renege on their promise when they encounter slight setbacks.

We should bear in mind that it is wrong to whinge about one's job as one is doing it. The success in any job comes from much effort and energy. You can get on the path to success only if you are willing to think, work hard and find real joy in your work. This is the secret to progress. Otherwise, you will be looking at *that* hill while sitting on *this* hill, thinking of *that* job while doing *this* job. You will spend your precious time arguing over what is right or wrong, what is gained or lost, unwilling to be serious and down-to-earth, and getting down to doing the work that you ought to be doing. As a result, you become restless, lazy and dispirited, encumbered even with the basic task of earning a living, let alone achieving great success and accomplishment.

"The grass is always greener on the other side" is the thinking of a glutton, an opportunist and a sloth. A person truly dedicated to his work will hold firm to his post. Only by so doing will he gain confidence, and with this self-confidence, win the trust of others!

Written on 17 April 1955 at Bedok Beach

14 A performance is "seven parts gong and three parts song"

One only performs solo if left with no choice. As long as one is offered the opportunity, one should always perform in concert with like-minded people with common aspirations. With more people working in concert, the brilliant and fast workers will be able to play more fully to their abilities, bringing their work to its peak.

A dream of success is very beautiful, but a large gap exists between one's dream and reality. Undoubtedly, success is contingent on one's intelligence and hard work, but we cannot neglect the role played by circumstances. A great poet who strives his whole life must still bow to the power of his circumstances. He thus says: "I cannot succeed on my own, my accomplishment is three parts the work of man, seven parts heaven's blessing." "The work of man" means individual intelligence and effort and "heaven's blessing" means being blessed with the right circumstances. This saying is more commonly expressed as "seven parts gong and three parts song". Although somewhat hackneyed, it contains a profound truth.

A successful stage show requires the tight collaboration of people both on- and off-stage. Should the show lack an excellent orchestra, the stage setting not be realistic, and the supporting cast not spontaneous in making room at every turn for the lead actors to shine, the lead actors can never perform at their best. As all the participants in a show (lead actors, supporting actors, extras, conductor, drummers, prop and lighting crew) have a substantial grasp of what the show is about and what is needed of them, all are willing to give of their best. This manifests in the rigorous preparation leading up to the show, the meticulous execution during the show, and the reflective post-performance evaluation, with everyone using his intelligence and passion to drive the show to success. Simply put, were there not so many unsung heroes working their heads off behind the scenes, the lead actors would be of no use.

Everyone can appreciate how "seven parts gong, and three parts song" applies in the context of performance. Why can't this principle be applied elsewhere? Let us take architecture for example: the Imperial Palace in Beijing is world famous because of its majestic style and grandeur and its use of exquisite, elegant materials. Every drop and spot, each bend and turn, every door, pillar and beam is built in accordance with established practices and standards, and yet in no way lacks freshness and ingenuity. Deserving of special notice are Tian'anmen Square and Chang'an Street, the Prospect Hill behind the Imperial Palace, the Tai Temple on the left (the present-day Beijing Working People's

Cultural Palace) and the Central Garden on the right (the present Beijing Zhongshan Park). While each site has its distinguishing feature, when all are lined up with the Imperial Palace, they come together to accentuate the palace's beauty. Furthermore, the high, thick walls of the Beijing city, the orderly streets, the squarish courtyards and the dense foliage foreground the magnificently glazed tiles of the Imperial Palace, making them stand out even more prominently.

Music and architecture might be understood as "seven parts gong and three parts song"; we need to take into account both the "backstage" and "background". Similarly, people who are doing research work cannot get away from a few academic centres. These academic centres have these requirements: they belong to the highest institutions; they are well-equipped with libraries and laboratories; they possess outstanding scholars. One can only find a few such academic centres in a country. Some countries may only have one such centre. People who are really serious in research work would rather stay in the academic centre and suffer from hunger than to go to a culturally-backward area to enjoy shark's fin and bird's nest. And why is this the case? Well, once a scholar leaves the academic centre, he will be like a fish out of water and become dispirited.

A person who grasps the principle of "seven parts gong and three parts song" will never again dare to show off his talent or blow his own trumpet. He knows very well that doing a one-man show is the last resort. At every opportunity, he will work with like-minded people with common aspirations. With more people working in concert, the brilliant and fast workers will be able to play more fully to their abilities, bringing their work to its peak.

In this era in which we optimise resource allocation, we focus on collective creation in all things. It is thus presumably not meaningless that I should discuss "seven parts gong and three parts song" at this time.

Written in the morning 9 January 1955

15   The moon at mid-autumn is especially bright

A person's spirit is high on a joyous occasion, the moon especially bright during the mid-autumn. In life, it is truly rare that one can be at ease with one's circumstances. Thus, on the occasion that we are situated comfortably, we ought to exploit it fully to bring into full play our wisdom and ability in order to achieve greater things.

There are twelve months in a year, but a full moon is not seen in the middle of every month, for it may sometimes be obscured by rain or fog, too chilly in the winter and too damp when spring is shifting into summer. After taking account of all these factors, it would seem that the only time of the year when the moon is really full is mid-autumn.

By the middle of the eighth lunar month, the deep-autumn air has grown cool and crisp, clouds are high and humidity low, with the fog having dissipated. In the cloudless sky above, a bright moon hangs singly in the air, enchanting, glistening; below, the play of dancing shadows serves further to enhance the brilliance of the moon.

The saying "The moon at mid-autumn is especially bright" has a profundity to it. It is a sign that when the time and circumstance are suitably matched, something special will take place. Conversely, when time and circumstance are out of joint, pursuing the same action will yield a different outcome.

Another common saying runs, "Contend for fame in the imperial capital, for profit in the marketplace." The capital of a nation is where diverse multitudes of people and resources gather, bringing with them their various talents. If you think that you excel in a particular field or skill, you should go to the capital to prove your skill or talent. In the capital are many respectable masters and critics with original insights; either could raise your profile tenfold should you win them over. To say the least, if you are willing to be humble, the capital will present you with a myriad opportunities to learn and improve. As long as you are not complacent or self-satisfied, you can always get help or learn from your seniors or contemporaries in your field of specialization. To receive help and be pointed in the right direction is like applying the vital touch that will cause one to enjoy the experience of "being lost, though not too far off-course; understanding what is done right today and the errors made the day before". From here, if you work hard, great achievement will eventually follow. This is far better than fumbling in the dark by yourself.

The principle of contending for profit in the marketplace is easier to understand. The modern metropolis is usually divided into residential, cultural, industrial, financial, business and administrative sectors. It makes sense that various banks should congregate to form the finance district, while department stores should ideally be situated next to each other to form an area of maximum catchment; customers enter one department store and exit via another, in a continuous retail experience. Furthermore, in a centralized market, stalls selling chicken, duck, fish, meat, vegetables, sundry goods and snacks are grouped together neatly in kind, each occupying a zone across the various floors. One would think that by arranging stalls that offer the same things in a cluster, the sales and profits of the stalls would be reduced. In reality, the reverse is true. Firstly, when shops selling similar merchandise are grouped together, they instantly form a specialty zone towards which customers would head when they have something in particular they want to buy, in the certainty that they will find satisfaction here. The volume of sales and trade in these centralized markets is many times higher than in isolated shops. Secondly, when shops in the same line of business are grouped in one place, they will save on administration and transportation costs when making collective purchases, resulting in lower costs. Thirdly, the only way modern businesses earn money, as prompted by the industrial practices of mass production, is to price themselves competitively but sell in bulk. With the increase in transactions in the modern centralized market, profits will be correspondingly large. And so, for one to run a modern enterprise, locating it in a prime, flourishing, spot is essential.

"The moon at mid-autumn is especially bright", the reason for which being that at mid-autumn, the time and circumstances coordinate perfectly to allow the moon to appear in her full splendor. Only in realising this principle might we then understand why a person would prefer to go to a noisy teahouse to chat with friends instead of staying home alone brewing a pot of tea, or why a person would go to a crowded library to do research instead of reading alone behind the closed doors of his room, or why a person is dissatisfied with training in a small ball-court and instead spends a great amount of money to observe and learn from national and international games. The reason is that in an environment when the time and circumstances are well-matched, a person will be excited, inspired and motivated. We should know that a hardworking person may not necessarily achieve his expected goal, but one who does not work has no hope at all. A person's spirit is high on a joyous occasion, the moon especially bright during the mid-autumn. In life, it is truly rare that one can be at ease with one's circumstances. Thus, on the occasion that we are situated comfortably, we ought to exploit it fully to bring into full play our wisdom and ability in order to achieve greater things.

16 One can not become a doctor after taking medicine for three years

No matter how reliable a guide is or how intricate our tools are, direct experience is still needed, and things need to be mulled over repeatedly before we can understand the difficulties involved. Only then will we have real growth and learning.

The saying that "prolonged illness makes a doctor of a patient", or that "one can become a doctor after taking medicine for three years", encapsulates the idea that sustained experience increases one's wisdom.

It has always been the case that to see something once is better than to hear of it a hundred times; it is even better to do something once than see it done a hundred times. Only when one actually start doing a thing does one comprehend the difficulties involved; only then can there be real growth and learning.

The human race took a huge step forward when it shifted from raw to cooked food, from cooked food to seasoning, and from blending flavours to preparing good wine and cuisines. Illness finds its way into one's body through the mouth, so gluttony increases one's chance of falling ill. When one is ill, one's family will need to find one a cure. In the past, there were neither doctors nor pharmacies, much less hospitals. Some intelligent person in the past tasted hundreds of plants and learnt which herb was good for what kinds of illnesses, and which was useless. All his observations were methodically recorded. Upon next encountering the same kind of illness, the same medicinal herb could be used. Subsequently, as the human population increased and the social system became more complex, Man started practicing specialisation; it was now unnecessary for everyone to taste hundreds of plants, this job being entrusted to the select few who became professionals in medical care. The sick would consult a doctor, who issued prescriptions to the patients, who then purchased the medicines from the pharmacy. It is now no longer necessary to prepare one's own medicine using raw materials. Such strides we have made since olden times!

Why do we say that "prolonged illness makes a doctor of a patient" or that "one can become a doctor after taking medicine for three years"? Normally, time passes swiftly when one is comfortable and doing well. However, when one is ill, all activities come to a halt; a day draws out and feels like a year when one is lying in bed endlessly with nothing to look forward to except a slew of medicines. During this period of boredom and loneliness, all patients desire a speedy recovery. To pass the time, the illiterate makes detailed inquiries of the doctor; over time his medical knowledge increases. Meanwhile, a literate person can pore over medical books, consulting the doctors when in doubt, and applying what he has learnt. Over time, and through trial and error, he arrives at an understanding of various illnesses and medicine. In these time of modern medical advancement, one has to study for six or seven years before receiving a medical degree. However, back in the days when medicine was in its infancy, one could be a doctor by studying medical books for three years or just by having two to three years of clinical practice.

I cannot help thinking of the Doctor of Philosophy (PhD) when we mention the term "doctor". A person with a doctorate has greater access to resources and opportunities than one without;once such a person enters society, he is usually given an important position and a handsome salary. This kind of preferential treatment towards people who has not worked for it, more often than not, makes many with doctorates become good-for-nothings in life. As they take up high positions right from the start, they are insufferably arrogant, not deigning to handle many matters personally. Their lack of experience and inability to appreciate the difficulties involved cause them to issue commands indiscriminately and reproach others thoughtlessly, generating dissonance and constant strife. There exists a saying in the workplace "a genius at twenty, a pain in the neck at fifty". This is by no means a fault of the PhD; rather, it is the mistake of those who have the qualification but fail to use it wisely.

If a person who has already excelled academically is willing to begin with the fundamentals in his career, without lazily taking shortcuts, his future will know no limits. Knowledge from books is at best the essence of the experiences of our predecessors; without direct experience, we will be unable to understand the difficulties involved, and what one claims to know can only be at most an echo of what one's predecessors said.

"One should learn how to row before trying to take the rudder." This saying is especially meaningful to those aspiring to succeed. An inexperienced person is flustered and muddled in the face of crises. Conversely, an experienced person is able to turn a situation around and handle the crisis with ease.

I acknowledge that the knowledge gained from books is the accumulated wisdom of millenia. It serves as our guide and may spare us the pain of groping in the dark; it is also an excellent tool able to save us much effort. But, to be frank, no matter how reliable a guide is or how intricate our tools are, direct experience is still needed, and things need to be mulled over repeatedly before we can understand the difficulties involved. Only then will we have real growth and learning.

Written in early morning, 16 January 1955

17 How much joy is travelling

> *"There will always be another mountain higher than this." If you want to know whether the mountain you are on is high enough, you need to travel widely in order to make a meaningful comparison.*

A person who spends the whole day in the office poring over routine chores is like a donkey tethered to a mill; its familiarity with the route allows it to pace the course with its eyes closed. But the lack of variation and stimulation leaves him numbed, and needless to say, this is a loss. In truth, if you can strike a balance between work and rest, your efficiency at work will certainly improve.

Engaging with activities is a better way to relax than passively reposing. People who spend long hours in the office and live in heavily populated cities have very few opportunities for physical activity. The best way to spend the weekends is thus to picnic in the countryside, swim, hike, play ball games, or at least go to a nearby park to stretch and breathe in the wild scents of nature. Of course, the best plan during the long holidays is to travel overseas.

In the same way that it is not easy to encounter a peerless beauty, it is difficult to find many breathtaking scenic spots. Given that Singapore is only a small island, it is unsurprising that not many scenic spots are to be found. When abroad, however, it is a very different kettle of fish. Though both offer spectacular sea views, the Mediterranean beaches inspire romance while the Atlantic Ocean awes you into solemn contemplation.

Though both offer mountain views, the Oriental landscape is dotted with bamboo fences and hay-thatched cottages, with little bridges over trickling streams, while that of the West sports well-trimmed evergreens and cottages with colourfully painted roofs and walls. As the saying goes: "There will always be another mountain that is higher than this." If you want to know whether the mountain you are on is high enough, you need to travel widely in order to make a meaningful comparison.

Given current improvements in transportation, travel has become extremely convenient. I often say that the citizen-as-diplomat is more important than official diplomacy. Official diplomacy is often glib and insincere, while diplomacy, as conducted by the citizen, is open and honest. Should a person wish to learn more about the people and customs of another country, he should never depend solely on official statistics or conversations with government officials. He should meet instead with middle or working-class locals to get a sense of the way things really are, and extensive traveling is the shortcut to acquiring that sense.

There is a good deal of truth in the saying, "It is better to see once than hear a hundred times," for many things which seem incomprehensible may become clear when seen with one's own eyes. Should there still be things that remain inscrutable even after scrutiny, persistent inquisitiveness will eventually help one arrive at a complete understanding. In today's world, those in power understand the value of travel, frequently sending experts abroad on study-tours, with the country reaping great rewards in various aspects within a short time.

Not only does traveling promote friendship and enhance one's knowledge, it also brings much gastronomic satisfaction. While we love our local flavours, unless we personally experience the local wine and specialities of other lands, we will forever be unacquainted with their flavour. We could invite the chefs from afar, but it would pose some difficulty to acquire the authentic ingredients, and utterly impossible to move over the scenery from these faraway places. Only when we taste certain foods in situ, and with the right ambience, can we truly appreciate the goodness of the dish. Even the most exquisite delicacy loses its flavour without the right context and ambience.

The pleasures of travel are many. However, travel needs money, fairly strong legs and pleasant company. A group might number four or five, or just comprise a couple. Large travel groups would spoil all the fun, for only the few people in front would be able to see anything, those at the back missing out on most of the views or explanations being given by the guide. This is especially true when visiting factories or other organizations. Should it not be possible to get a suitable companion, traveling alone is in truth not a bad option. In any case, transportation today is very easy and travel agencies abound in all the large cities. Today, a stranger in a strange land would have no worries about food and lodging, as long as he had money.

My resolution for the coming year is to read and write more; at the same time, I shall tighten my purse strings and cut down on my expenditure. When I have enough for my travel expenses, I shall apply for vacation from my company to go traveling. I am very sure the money will be well-spent.

Written at Christmas 1954

18   There is no greater joy than making new friends

Friends are loveable. They are your mirrors and salt in life. A true friend, however, is really hard to come by.

"There is no greater sadness than to be separated by death, no greater joy than to find a new friend." As attested to by this quotation from *"Nine Songs"* (Jiu Ge) by the great Chinese poet Qu Yuan, the most painful experience in life is to be separated from a loved one by death, while the greatest happiness lies in having found someone who understands your innermost thoughts.

Familial relations—whether parents, children, brothers or sisters—are a wholly genetic matter. We may be friends with family members, but not always so. Well over two or three thousand years ago, folk poets among us had suggested: "While Brotherhood exists, far superior is Friendship." This saying points out that having a brother who is not like-minded pales in comparison to a friend who is willing to lay bare his heart and mind.

Indeed, nothing is of greater concern in life than survival. Apart from the wealthy, the vast majority of humanity strive daily just to provide for themselves and their families. The able survive, the unfit perish; it is that simple. It is indeed rare for someone to offer to share his sustenance with you. Only a handful of friends are able to help you materially; even fewer are those with whom one is able to commune spiritually. This is especially true with respect to accomplished academics and artists, considering that they stand at the lonely pinnacles of their fields, on a level where a bosom friend is but infrequently encountered. Thus, these lonely souls drift upon the sea of humanity, forlorn and companionless.

In life, someone who has mentored or guided you on the path to success may of course be considered a bosom friend. Someone who encourages you in your studies or helps you further your career is clearly a dear friend too. The closeness is even more pronounced in a relation in which friendship is mingled with tutelage, when one is willing to impart one's experience and hand over the secrets to success, in the hope of seeing the other succeed him.

It is already fortuitous for a fresh graduate to encounter a supervisor who appreciates his abilities and singles him out for grooming; rarer still is it that one is able to find a handful of comrades in study or work who look out for one another, hone and enhance each other's abilities. When one has attained success in life, the mission of identifying and grooming the younger generation to whom the mantle may be passed ultimately depends on the ability to discern the uncommonly gifted, and even luck.

Let us now explore the ways of building friendship. R. W. Emerson once said, "The only way to *have* a friend is to *be* one." The ancient Chinese philosopher Lao tzu also taught, "To receive, first give." The best practice is for one to offer help to a friend who is in urgent need even before one is asked. Offering help only when your friend requests it makes you a mediocre friend. And to haggle and negotiate when your friend is asking you for help is to relegate yourself to the lowest level of friendship.

"Giving" should be done freely and willingly, while one should "receive" modestly, not exploitatively. For instance, should you only ask a modicum of what your friend is capable of, he would be able to accomplish the request effortlessly. On the other hand, should you be too demanding, stretching your friend to the limit, things will surely turn ugly for both parties, with one you accusing the other of being too stingy, and your friend blaming you for being overly demanding. It is not worth jeopardising the friendship like this.

While having many friends is a joy in life, having too many causes your time and energy to be spread very thin. Much of your precious time will be expended in chatting with these friends or socialising. In the interests of conserving time and energy, one should observe a strict discipline in the number of friends one makes. After all, mere acquaintances will cause you to fritter away your time and energy, and they are of no consequence to your studies and career. Instead of indiscriminately befriending acquaintances, one should guard oneself carefully and cultivate a proper friendship with the knowledgeable and able few.

In all honesty, friends are loveable. They are your mirrors and salt in life. A true friend, however, is really hard to come by; this is because friendship has to be mutual, dependant on the compatibility of both parties' interests, abilities and hobbies. Many have gone through life without a single close friend. Hence the saying "Many are acquaintances, but few are intimates" is still relevant and much quoted today.

Written at New Year 1955

19   True beauty comes from within

> *Good health is not only the foundation of all happiness, but is almost synonymous with beauty. Beauty increases as health improves. One must attain the highest level of health in order to achieve the highest level of beauty.*

It is human to adore beauty, but true beauty comes from nature. Look, the capricious clouds in the sky, the flowers in the garden blooming in a riotous blaze of colours, the myriad species of birds and animals in the wild, or the fantastic creatures submerged in the watery depths, none of their unique floral patterns or dazzling hues artificially enhanced, but all of them worthy of our admiration and enjoyment. The world may say "Man needs to dress up, in the same way that figures of Buddha are decked out in gold", but no matter how scented and colourful the cosmetics, how fashionable the outfit or dazzling the jewellery, these things simply constitute superficial appearances and do not comprise the true self. One can only find the self's true beauty in nature, and natural beauty lies in the beauty of one's health.

The British writer J. Leigh Hunt once said, "The groundwork of all happiness is health." The American essayist R.W. Emerson also wrote, "Health is the condition of wisdom, and cheerfulness, its sign". In truth, a person should choose to live simply and stay healthy, rather than enjoy a luxurious but unhealthy lifestyle. You might not normally be conscious of health; it is only when you are ill that you will appreciate its value. You will fail to enjoy the good wine and sumptuous meals spread before you, the beautiful music sounding in your ears; you cannot travel to drink in the breathtaking sights of the world.

Instead, you will be confined in the hospital the whole day, whiling away precious time. It is when you are caught in such a situation that you begin to appreciate the truth expressed by the saying "the groundwork of all happiness is health".

Good health is not only the foundation of all happiness, but is almost synonymous with beauty. Beauty increases as health improves. One must attain the highest level of health in order to achieve the highest level of beauty.

How should one maintain good health? The question is a profound one, but might perhaps be addressed simply by "Walking is as good as riding; eating only when one is hungry can turn simple food into delicious fare".

We know that exercise is important because exercise speeds up metabolism and cleanses the blood. However, all exercises carry their own benefits and risks, especially when it comes to extreme sports. You only need to be careless just once for an accident to occur. The only risk-free exercise with everything to gain is strolling.

Just as important is our diet. Most people mistakenly consider frequent feasting to be the joy of life. In the first place, the dishes served at banquets are too excessive both in variety and the number of courses for the stomach to digest them properly. Furthermore, most banquets drag on for at least two to three hours, during which the stomach is continuously filled with salty, sour, bitter and spicy food, thus placing a great burden on it. In fact, apart from food that provides essential nutrition, such as milk, eggs, vegetable and fruits, having simple, light meals is far better than feasting on rich cuisine. While nutritious food may aid digestion, rich fare weakens the process. Since sickness enters the body through the mouth, as long as we guard our mouths closely, all our gastro-intestinal illnesses will disappear.

Lastly, the best way to maintain good health is to eliminate stress, to be confident and robust in one's physical and mental well-being. There is much truth in the saying, "He who believes himself well will be well." Despite the advances in medical technology, even brilliant surgeons believe in psychotherapy, because having a sound mind can have great benefits for the body.

Good health is the source of happiness and a prerequisite for beauty. To the young men and women in search of beauty: rather than squander your means on make-up, focus instead on preserving and improving your health. As the saying goes: "True beauty comes from within, not without." I am not writing in jest; there is truth in this.

Written late at night, 26 February 1955

20   The soaring melody halts the fleeting clouds

> *Besides the core subjects in the school curriculum, we should pay special attention to music. By putting equal emphasis on music and studies, we may strike a balance between exertion and relaxation. I believe that under the aesthetic and purifying influence of music, we will become better people, and our lives more meaningful.*

Who is playing the flute in the painted chamber?
Snatches of music borne on intermittent wind.
The soaring melody halts the fleeting clouds,
While clear, cold, moonlight shines through the curtains.
— (Tang Dynasty) Zhao Gu, *Listening to the Flute*

Long before humans invented the written word, they already knew how to speak, and above all, sing. Labourers would naturally grunt "heave ho", "heave ho", while they lifted heavy timber or rocks with calloused limbs. During a larger operation, the supervisor would ringingly begin a song, this naturally echoed by the rest of the crew. Their voices would rise and fall in succession, as they moved along in rhythmic step. Although the labour was hard and sweaty, their spirits were lifted and steps lightened after the simple sing-along. In contrast, had they kept their heads bowed and toiled away sulkily, they would probably only have been half as efficient.

Similarly, it was bleak and onerous work for farmers working in the wild and melancholic mountains, cutting wood, plucking mulberry and picking tea leaves. To raise their spirits and boost morale, villagers occasionally gave voice in joyful, loud tones. These primitive, heartfelt songs resonated unexpectedly with the fellow compatriots in the mountains, enjoining them to join in this unceasing song. This lent them courage and dispelled the fear of poisonous snakes and wild animals in the jungle; at the same time, their spirits were lifted and comforted, the hillsongs even becoming love songs, as they wooed the other at work.

In fact, the great educators of ancient China knew the importance of music. Under the Confucian pedagogy of the Six Arts, the emphasis both on music and physical education combined to outweigh the later system in which only reading, writing and mathematics had been given weight. Modern medicine professes that the way to longevity is relaxation, and the way to relaxation through music. The best results are obtained if you can play a musical instrument or two; if not, listening to the radio or music player also helps you forget all your cares. As a last resort, if you neither play an instrument nor possess a radio or sound system, you might belt it out lustily while showering in the evening. Just sing in any way you like and let all the injustice and unhappiness drain away with your singing.

Music is not only an effective way whereby to balance your heart and mind but also the best way to make friends. Many so-called friends in the world out there are mostly hypocrites; they address each other as brothers but gripe and gossip behind each other's backs. All these are honestly rather difficult to bear. Music, however, is different. It is the pure voice from the heart, the untainted tone of the soul. There is much hypocrisy in society but not in music. One who truly understands music will always be happy and fulfilled.

Our young people should not spend the whole day studying. Not only is this bad for the body, but the mind will also lack room to unwind. We hope that our friends in the music industry will sacrifice some of their time and energy to take the initiative to help our young people in this respect. We promise unstinting support to any healthy entertainment programs or event that they might organize, whether for instrumental or vocal music.

Indeed, playing or singing a song is sometimes much more powerful than speaking a thousand words. Imagine, on a night lit by a high and brilliant moon: "A single note sounds from the distant flute; one leans enchanted against the balustrade." How mesmerizing an image this is! Imagine yet again: as you return from a picnic in the balmy dusk, suddenly you hear the singing from across the river but see no one. "The melody draws to a close with no singer in sight, leaving only the mountain peaks silently reflected in the river." Such poetic ambience is rendered poignant mostly by the powers of music.

Besides the core subjects in the school curriculum, we should pay special attention to music. By putting equal emphasis on music and studies, we may strike a balance between exertion and relaxation. I believe that under the aesthetic and purifying influence of music, we will become better people, and our lives more meaningful.

Written on 19 July 1959

21 The flowers and trees I planted form a little path

Though he lived in a prosperous era, he already understood fully the value of labour. Wherever possible, he worked hard to earn a living, never taking advantage of others. In fact, the momentary rest after labouring tasted especially sweet to him.

Were you to ask me to point out a respectable politician-cum-literati in the history of China, I would assuredly name Wang Anshi first. Even though Wang devoted his whole life to writing and working in the imperial court, his private life was very interesting. When he was away on retreat living in Jinling, he wrote this poem:

> The ground under the thatched eaves is clean-swept and free of moss,
> The flowers and trees I planted form a little path.
> A protective stream surrounds the field of green,
> While two mountains greet me at the door with their verdancy.

This poem reflects the painstaking efforts Wang took to tend to his garden. Although the ground under the thatched eaves was usually untidy with weeds here, and rubbish there, Wang's frequent cleaning and scrubbing left no chance for moss to grow. People of some social standing would normally leave the hard work of gardening to the workers and not bother themselves with it. They would be indifferent to whether the flowers bloomed or wilted, or if the plants lived or died. Wang took care of all the gardening himself, and so after ten years of diligent nurturing, the flowers and trees imperceptibly flourished, with the space between the plants turning into a little path.

There is another way of looking at Wang Anshi's poem. I am not too concerned with the last two lines about the scenery but would rather focus on the first two lines about how diligently he cleaned the ground and attended to the plants. In other words, these lines suggest that Wang Anshi, who made it his career to topple the unreasonable old systems in the imperial court, had long since proposed and practised the slogan "Labour is sacred".

Confucianism had been a belief that supported the ruling class and advocated keeping things as they were, and which thus incurred the ire of the common people. Once, Confucius asked his favourite disciple Zi Lu to ask for directions. An uncouth farmer gave him a talking to and said, "You never use your limbs to work, nor can you differentiate the five grains, yet you call yourselves teachers?" The farmer was apparently venting all his pent-up frustrations and indignation on the unfortunate Zi Lu.

Wang Anshi was a prime minister during the Song dynasty as well as one of the literati. An unrefined person in his position would have been smug and complacent, but not Wang. Even though he had to support about fifty or sixty relatives and friends, he only drew for himself a humble salary. It is most rare that even though he lived in a prosperous era, he already understood fully the value of labour. Whenever possible, he worked hard to earn a living, never taking advantage of others. In fact, the moments rest taken after laboring tasted especially sweet to him. The two lines from his poem, "The ground under the thatched eaves is swept clean and free of moss. The flowers and trees I planted form a little path" prove that Wang Anshi was not merely mouthing the slogan, but was taking real action in order to derive true joy.

In socialist societies, there exists no such classes of people as those who only work and those who only enjoy themselves. In other words, everyone has to work and learn. Working and learning are inseparable, for only then will workers be interested in their work, which in turn will raise productivity and yield outstanding results. In their leisure time, they are able to get involved in cultural recreations—singing, dancing and generally enjoying themselves to their hearts' content. In ancient times, some people would devote themselves to enjoyment while others would be forced to toil and labour; some would be stuffed with food yet others would starve to death; some would lead a bored and idle life while others would be kept busy with labour and work… Such was the great divide in their lifestyles.

When I read this poem by Wang Anshi thirty-five years ago in my hometown, I was able to recite it after just a glance, though I could not quite glean its significance. It was not until after I started work and read books on economics and socialism that I came to appreciate the true meaning of the verse "The flowers and trees I planted form a little path".

Written on 8 May 1955 late at night

22   Contentment is found when sought in serenity

> *"Contemplation" is not a denial of reality; rather it is a form of planned preparation for "serenity". When you are calm, your mind is focused, your consciousness is heightened, and you can always see more deeply into matters than others.*

Naught can vex a mind at ease,
Which slumbers till the east is crimson-tinged.
Contentment in serenity is found,
And pleasure in all seasons doth abound. ①
    — (Song Dynasty) Cheng Hao, *Incidental Creation (Ou Cheng)*

    The four lines are extracted from a poem by the Song Dynasty poet, Cheng Hao (Cheng Mingdao). The most important phrase, one deserving of further meditation is "Contentment in serenity is found".
    With rapid urbanization and increasing population density, the idea of "serenity" is rapidly vanishing. The city is characterized by hustle and bustle, noise and chaos. Apart from the wealthiest businessmen and

powerful government officials, the middle-lower income families live in crowded, spartan apartments, travel by way of public transport packed like sardines, and dine in public eateries swarming with other families. Their work place is filled with the clatter of the typewriter and computer keyboards, and punctuated by the ring of the telephone. Those working in factories have to suffer the rumble of motors and machines whirling up and down, a deafening cacophony at once monotonous and nerve-wracking.

Man is by nature a product of his environment: we react in certain ways in particular environments, and react differently when the circumstances change. Confucius once said: "The wise enjoy the waters, the benevolent, the mountains. The wise are active, the benevolent, placid. The wise are happy, the benevolent live long." Leaving the definitions of the "wise" and the "benevolent" aside for now, we know that the majority of those who prefer living in the mountains are quiet people, and because of their love of quiet, they get to enjoy a long life. Most of the people who prefer living by the sea are active people, and because of their activity, their lives are more vibrant, and they are far more likely than city-dwellers to enjoy life more fully.

The "contemplative" person is one who is contented; a contented person will not be covetous. Zhuangzi was such a person. According to the records of *Shi Ji*, King Wei of the Kingdom of Chu heard of Zhuangzi's outstanding abilities and specially sent envoys to present Zhuangzi with many gifts so as to entice him to be his Prime Minister. Any other person in that situation would inevitably have shed tears of elation. However, Zhuangzi refused the invitation. Had he not been habitually practicing "serene contemplation", I believe he would not have displayed such indifference to fame and fortune.

I often feel that the two phrases that Zhuge Liang penned in a letter to his son: "One can have no clear vision without indifference to worldly gains, one can accomplish little without peace of mind", were the most powerful guiding principles in his life. People who do not live simply, but instead strive daily for fame and wealth and indulge in various cardinal vices will, over time, abandon all their aspirations. People lacking an attitude of serenity will only have a skin-deep understanding of all things and are prone to self-congratulate; such people are eager for short-term gain and are without greater ambitions. Zhuge Liang loved his son so much that he handed down this most cherished bit of wisdom of his life to his son, hoping that his son would not go astray.

"Contemplation" is not a denial of reality; rather it is a form of planned preparation for "serenity". When you are calm, your mind is focused, your consciousness is heightened, and you can always see more deeply into matters than others. In fact, the person who is truly able to attain "serene contemplation" will have a heart as clear as a mirror. The beauty or ugliness of the external world are reflected in that mirror.

Should a person's heart not be serene enough, even somewhat restless, it will be like a dust-covered mirror, its image wavering, with the external world no longer reflected clearly.

A serene mind is the secret to a healthy life. It develops your mind and prolongs your life. Spending the day in a troubled and restless state of mind results in your feeling fatigued by day's end, but yet being without the ability to sleep well at night. Should you lead this kind of life, you will experience your days as years, feeling half dead. A person who practises serene contemplation will have a positive outlook on life and an accurate perception of causes and effects, distinguish between what is superficial and of essential, right and wrong, gains and losses. Why would a person like this deign to argue with another over trivialities?

A tranquil environment can impart a sense of serenity within a person, who in turn beautifies the world around him. Only under such circumstances will one experience freedom and contentment in all things.

Written on February 6, 1955 at dawn

Notes:

① These four lines of poetry by Cheng Hao express the feeling that when one is at peace, one is unhurried in all that one does. When one awakens, the red sun has risen high over his east-facing window. Through contemplating all things calmly, one can derive the joys of nature; such is the sensation of all men who drink in the wonderful scenery of the seasons all year round.

The ending four lines of this seven-character poem read: "This truth permeates all things in life, transpiring even in the winds of change. Merry are the poor, untouched by the lure of riches; such is the mantle of a true hero."

23 Stealing half a day of bliss from the rush of life

> *A person must know how to make use of his leisure time to engage in activities that strengthen his body and mind. If one congregates regularly to engage in frivolous chat, or fills the belly but starves the mind all day long, his leisure time becomes a burden instead.*

In my short essay titled "Fame crowns not the lazy head", I advised young people to be hardworking; as an antithesis, I now propose this topic: "Stealing half a day of bliss from the bustle of life", emphasising the importance of "leisure". On the surface, it would seem that I am contradicting myself; in fact, the two things are interlinked and not mutually exclusive.

Whether you are working or studying, the word "lazy" should not appear in your lexicon, while the word "leisure" should definitely be included. While the word "lazy" has only negative connotations, "leisure" carries a positive inflection. On the one hand, it benefits both body and mind occasionally to unwind the normally high-strung nerves with half a day's break for leisure. On the other, the office worker who handles routine chores in the company is not too different from a talking machine; he might be busy all day long but fails to acquire any new experience or knowledge. Such a person is badly in need of half a day of relaxation, so that his brain may revive from its inert state. Rest and nourishment will enable him to cope better with difficult problems at work the following day.

As the saying goes: "There is no trouble under the sun, until the foolish one stirs it up himself." How true this is! The ordinary man tries to outsmart himself most of the time, but eventually blows things out of all proportion, and fusses over the mess thus created, resulting in nary a day of peace. He should try to stop fussing over nothing, and instead spare some time in meditating, or read books that broaden his perspective; perhaps this will save society from much dispute!

The ancients advocated "self-reflection in the silence of the night" and to "examine one's own heart", but these are definitely not what those who are preoccupied with work round the clock can practise. Busy people simply lack proper time for contemplation, their motto being "work", "work", "work"; and when things go wrong, they start blaming others while completely shirking their share of responsibility. If they could invest a little time in evaluating the rights and wrongs, loss and gains, many unnecessary disputes could be avoided.

No matter how busy a person is, he should know to squirrel away moments of leisure, this especially true for politicians and industrialists, who are busy handling affairs all day long, vetting documents, planning, chairing meetings and hosting guests. However, no matter how busy he is, a first-rate politician will always know how to steal a moment of leisure in which to engage in self-cultivation.

The legendary British Prime Minister Winston Churchill knew very well how to preserve a moment of leisure from the rush of his bustling life. While having to look into a myriad matters every day, he still made a little time in which to catnap, being then much invigorated when he awoke. The fact is, we can be strongly interested in anything only when we are excited; with this strong interest aroused, we can then excel in anything we set ourselves to. No wonder that he excelled in all that he attempted, whether literature, military, politics, foreign languages or painting. He picked up sculpture only when he was 81, which shows that people who knows how to sneak in moments of leisure are those who best know how to enjoy life.

A person must know how to make use of his leisure time to engage in activities that strengthen his body and mind. If one congregates regularly to engage in frivolous chat, or fills the belly but starves the mind all day long, his leisure time becomes a burden instead. When a person needs to spend more energy and effort to engage in "boring pastimes", the meaningfulness of leisure has been utterly lost.

It is no easy task to "steal half a day of leisure from the rush of life" while living in a busy city. Apart from stealing breaks in our daily grind to engage in meaningful tasks, we should also schedule at least half a day for leisure every week, for nothing harmful will ever come from a well-planned break.

Written on May 22, 1955 late at night

24   The hair grows pale but the colour of one's native accent is unfading

> *A particularly comprehensive Mother Tongue education supplies a person with the fine tools of expression and expressiveness, while at the same time, equipping him with the skills and means by which to establish and conduct himself in the world.*

Another term for "native speech" is "parent language" or "mother tongue". The heart of an infant growing up in his mother's tender cradle is a joyous one; at this stage, too, his ability to imitate is exceptionally strong. The moment the infant is exposed to speech from his first year or so, he echoes his mother's manner of speaking. By the time he has reached his fourth or fifth year, he is already capable of switching fluidly between a variety of grammatical structures and tones. His vocabulary and idiomatic mastery increase from day to day. Unless he be relocated to a completely different environment before the age of 10 and made to acquire another language or dialect from scratch, his deep, pronounced, local accent will never change.

My friend Liu Gongyun highly approves of Han Suyin's (or Elisabeth Comber) gift for literary work in English . He says: "(Only) Han Suyin's English feels properly English in flavour". But Han Suyin herself has this to say: "That I could make a good fist of writing in English is due to my strength in Chinese." Her remark is not meant to be provocative but is, rather, rooted in facts. Chiang Yee both made a living and a name for himself in English. Of his over 20 published works—discounting a handful which document his travel around the world under the pseudonym of "The Mute Wanderer"—his more substantial writings not only drew from Chinese sources for their setting, but in essence employ English whereby to discuss Chinese calligraphy and aesthetics. Moreover, the illustrations in his books are rendered using pure Chinese brushwork, this being, without a doubt, a novelty for foreign readers.

While I stress the significance of one's "accent" or Mother Tongue, I am not against the study of foreign languages. What I am arguing for is precisely that which is propounded by Han Wengong, that "there is a rightful order to understanding any principle, proper specialisation in every skill and discipline". In other words, those of Chinese origin should first master Chinese, and only after, surplus energy permitting, English too. Were those of Chinese origin first to master English, or worse still, dismiss Chinese, this would not only predispose him to incur the contempt of the wise and discerning foreigner, but, further, cause him to lose his cultural bearings in societies in which Chinese and other influences are commingled.

Switzerland springs naturally to mind while we are on the topic of learning a Mother Tongue. The matter of linguistic communities in Switzerland is a very complicated one. All its formal (or official) documentation is written in German, French and Italian. In the eyes of the law, everyone regardless of nationality, is equal. Every community has its own dialect school; after a child has mastered his Mother Tongue, he proceeds to learn his second, third, and even fourth language. Switzerland, in relation to international politics, maintains a neutral front, while domestically, everyone is treated equitably, this accounting for what is arguably the most exemplary manifestation of law and order in all Europe.

A two-lined Chinese proverb reads: "The son does not dislike the mother's ugliness, the dog does not despise the house's poverty." These lines best exemplify the greatness of Chinese culture and the richness of its folk customs and social mores.

It has been 30 years since I left my hometown. I admit that my hometown was a poor, remote village. I admit too that my hometown was stifling, provincial and culturally impoverished. But my hometown has blessed me with a healthy body, with a compassionate disposition, and further, with an indomitable will, and a forward-looking, optimistic spirit. These are the only resources I may depend on as I strike out into the world.

"The hair grows pale but one's native accent is unchanged." He who recites this line of verse should take pride in himself, for even as merciless time ensures he ages every day, one's way of speaking remains steadfast and unchanging. A particularly comprehensive Mother Tongue education supplies a person with the fine tools of expression and expressiveness, while at the same time, equipping him with the skills and means by which to establish and conduct himself in the world. Education has always been the means whereby one's innate ability is brought into full play; the aim of education is achieved if its appropriate administration brings out one's good conscience and fully develop one's talents. To "shave the foot to fit the shoe①", to belittle the worth of one's Mother Tongue, and to despise one's accent or native speech—all of these practices I would not dare to entertain.

Written September 4th, 1955 in a hotel in Donghai

Notes:

① This means to force-fit or accommodate inappropriately.

25   A general's glory, ten thousand bodies

> *War is a cursed thing; it rends a man from his parents, siblings and wife. It causes buildings of historical importance to be burnt to ashes, suppresses the purity of Man's nature, and brings into full play his combative and beastly part of his nature. Those who take part in wars – of ten who go, nine fail to return.*

The rivers and mountains of Ze are drawn into the war maps,
The people are happy to chop wood and cut grass for a living
Cease to talk about promotion;
A general's glory, ten thousand bodies. ①
　　　　　　— (Tang Dynasty) Cao Song, *36 years old*

　　As I declaimed this Tang poem, suddenly, everything before me turned dizzyingly dark, there was a humming in my ears and all my hair stood on end. I remember the newspaper report on the first atomic bomb thrown from the sky; every house and every person within 12 km^2 was obliterated.

The improvement of military weapons, urbanisation and the growth in population have caused the "market-rate" of heroism to rise steeply. During those periods when people fought with bow and arrow, tens of thousands of lives were sacrificed for one general's glory. In an age when warfare is conducted with firearms, the "price to pay" for an admiral or commander-in-chief's achievement has gone up at least a hundredfold. In World War I, 13 million soldiers perished, 33 million commoners were killed and injured; on these two counts alone, the number of people dead and injured already totals 46 million, and this not even including the orphans, widows, prisoners-of-war and refugees. On average, the cost of a general's victory is measured in tens of thousands of lives and spirits. Based on the current state of military technology and demographic concentration, the "price to pay" for a land, sea or air general may clearly be expected to rise.

As far back as 30 to 40 years ago, there were many bandits in China. The military officials sent out their forces to round them up and suppress them. The bandits were unable to resist the police and surrendered to the officials, crossing over to their side to become their men. Not long after, due to devastating food shortages, these soldiers clamoured to become bandits again. With rifle in hand, one can become a soldier or bandit as the occasion demands. It is the common people who suffer from this lawless slippage between the soldiers and the bandits.

With the tightening of social groups and the elevation of the authority of law, the word of military officials becomes law. Should they conscript the citizen, he has no means of resistance. While there is always a noble reason for fighting a war, the reason is all the more seductive when politics change and the enemy turns into friendly forces. I often say that people who dabble in the military, politics, economics, diplomacy, publicity need always to be armed with two sides of the argument , using the affirmative when in agreement with some kind of policy, and negative when in disagreement with some other. Whether the policy is positive or negative, the policy-maker himself will never be wrong. On the other hand, all blunders had to be taken up by the citizen, every sacrifice borne by the people.

War in self-defence is still justifiable, but the wanton abuse of military might in order to invade is unpardonable. The heavens are disconsolate and nature sorrowful for those who suffered unjust deaths upon ancient battlefields. Their deaths were meaningless: other than having their bones and bodies become the stepping-stones for the various military officials and leaders, they gained nothing at all.

Having said that, the individual's resistance often yields little. What is most important is to gather all the resistance groups around the world which together might create an immensely sturdy stronghold of peace. Scientific inventions ought to be fully utilised for the purposes of keeping peace so as to raise the living standards of people all around the world, and with their remaining energy, people should conduct cultural exchanges to promote better understanding.

War is a cursed thing; it rends a man from his parents, siblings and wife. It causes buildings of historical importance to be burnt to ashes, suppresses Man's pure nature, and brings into full play his combative and beastly part of his nature. Those who take part in wars – of the ten who go, nine fail to return. In ancient times, women were exempted from military service, but in a society with gender equality, women are just as capable of treading the frontline, and are consequently unable to escape the perils of war.

We need only to examine carefully the famous line "A general's glory, ten thousand bodies" to fuel anti-war sentiment. Under the influence of such sentiments, it would be less easy to be naively led by the nose into an aggressive conflict.

Written on March 13th, 1955, in early morning

Notes:

① This means that in the imminence of war, the commoners are only too happy to be slogging away for their livelihood. Yet, even this supposed "happiness" can no longer be attained now.

26   How should I find ten thousand manors

> *It is only because Du Fu had endured a lifetime's worth of poverty which caused him to become homeless, and barely lived in a shabby thatched cottage, which was unluckily suffered from storm, that he was moved to utter the extravagant wish that he might build "thousands of high, spacious houses".*

One toils away from dawn to dusk while dwelling in a prosperous city, merely to meet the mundane demands for clothing, food, shelter and transportation.

Generally speaking, the problem of transportation is a relatively simple one to solve; you travel in a private conveyance if you are well-off, or public transport if poor. Even though travelling by public transport means having to halt along the way, and is thus more circuitous than a private vehicle, it nevertheless is capable of getting you to your destination. While one has to travel a little more before the trip begins and after it ends, not only is it not an impediment to health, it is, on the contrary, beneficial.

In the city, dining is also a casual affair. Permanent residents of Southeast Asia are not particular about what they eat. As long as the food carries the flavour of one's hometown, everyone would eat with gusto even if dining along the streets.

Meanwhile, the sartorial is a lot more carelessly treated in Singapore. With the exception of the minority fashionistas in Singapore, ordinary women can trot about the street informally dressed . As for men, even so-called average "white-collar worker" has long given up on ties, moving about dressed in a simple shirt.

Clothes, food, and travel are all easy to deal with, what is left—the problem of accommodation—is what one cudgels one's brain over the most.

Where Singapore are concerned, every inch of earth is worth a ton, and rental is very expensive. It is already difficult to find normal housing; the demand for hotels meant as tourist accommodation all the more outstrips supply. I remember on the 20th August 1937, I took my family away from under the iron heels of the oppressive Japanese forces occupying Beijing and spent a whole 14 hours before reaching Tianjin. After much difficulty, we finally found a shabby motel. Right after we put our luggage down, a heavy downpour followed and dripped continuously into the room. At that moment, I was brought to mind of how interesting Du Fu's "The Song of the Thatched Cottage Rent by the Autumn Wind" was. In particular, these two lines "How should I find ten thousand manors, in which to shelter and gladden all the homeless scholars[①]"—it was as though they had been specifically written with me in mind.

In cities where population is dense, the number of people growing sick tends to be particularly large. When a person is taken ill, he clearly has to seek a doctor. The cost of a private doctor is very high, and so only the middle to higher-income families can afford it. As the average to lower-income families cannot afford to visit a private doctor due to their economic condition, they can only seek medical advice from government hospitals. The number of patients seeking medical help in government hospitals tends to be overwhelming, with the waiting room crowded with people even before the doctor arrives. They only manage to see the doctor after waiting for half a day. The doctor's head is in a whirl while seeing patients, on the one hand listening to their medical conditions, and on another, unceasingly writing down the prescriptions. After receiving the prescription, the patient runs to the pharmacy to get his medication, but the pharmacy is itself also crowded, so he has to wait yet another half day to get his medicine. As suffering from a minor medical problem and going to government hospitals take up at least half a day, many of the less well-off patients mostly endure the suffering and brace themselves to go to work. Only when they have become incurably sick do they get sent by their family members to government hospitals where they stay over for observation.

The poetic line "How should I find ten thousand manors" sounds off a resoundingly bright note. It speaks of the exceptional aspirations of our great poet. Always selfless and impartial, he would rather sacrifice himself for a greater good. The line also casts light on how only the poor are best equipped to empathise with, and thus, best help, the other poor in this world.

It is only because Du Fu had endured a lifetime's worth of poverty which caused him to become homeless, and barely lived in a shabby thatched cottage, which was unluckily suffered from storm, that he was moved to utter the extravagant wish that he might build "ten thousand manors". A pity that "How should I" was appended to "ten thousand manors", this testifying to the great poet's fantasising, always at one remove from the real.

Written on 29th May 1955

Notes:

① "How should I find ten thousand manors, in which to shelter and gladden all the homeless scholars": taken from Du Fu's poem "The Song of the Thatched Cottage Rent by the Autumn Wind".

27 A stone that is fit for a wall is not left on the highway

> *A truly learned person has absolute faith in his future. Regardless of whether the circumstances are favourable or adverse, he will, nonetheless, with courage and determination, march on to realise his goals.*

While it is unnecessary to be arrogant, to overly belittle oneself is just as excessive. Arrogance is often annoying; self-belittlement, on the other hand, commonly invites pity.

In the view that "an honourable man should not accept sympathy from others", how can an individual with reasonable self-respect possibly permit others to pity him?

Rightfully, one's depth of knowledge and ability is fully dependent on and determined by one's talent and effort. Thus, a talented individual who is willing to put in his utmost effort will certainly be knowledgeable and very competent, this giving him sufficient self-assuredness to deal with matters as they come. That being said, whether a person is given a suitable opportunity to demonstrate his knowledge and ability still depends on whether the circumstances are favourable to him.

However, a truly learned person has absolute faith in his future. Regardless of whether the circumstances are favourable or adverse, he will, nonetheless, with courage and determination, march on to realise his goals. Staying true to one's own way and being at ease with it, he remains indifferent to worldly praise and criticism alike.

Li Bai of the Tang Dynasty was a great and highly intelligent poet, a free-spirited Romantic in character and disposition. Having noble aspirations, he despised those who fawned upon the powerful and flattered the rich, so as to build connections using underhanded and contemptible means. Therefore, in his classic "An Invitation to Toast", he bellowed unrestrainedly, "my god-given talents shall be employed; the thousand gold coins, scattered, will return". In fact, the line "my god-given talents shall be employed" is not mere drunken babble. The phrase suggests our great poet's conviction in his own future. We need to understand that an individual must possess confidence, and only then will he have the courage to persist; as long as he is willing to strive on, his future will be bright. Should his confidence falter and he not be willing to work hard, his future would look very bleak.

A religious follower will preach that at the very outset of any religion is the word "faith". With faith comes power and thus, the piety of a follower is the source of all his strength.

The great English author, Samuel Johnson (1709—1784) got it right: "Self-confidence is the first requisite to great undertakings." So it is indeed. Dr Johnson was a literary man, neither a renowned general, nor a strategist and definitely not a capitalist in possession of large fortune, and so he was not thought to have had a great career. However, he could take pride in his life as the first person to have compiled *A Dictionary of the English Language*. Before he embarked on his great undertaking of this compilation, he went to London to meet a famous man of his time. He waited for hours in the reception room but was ignored by the man. Ten years later, after eventually completing the compilation of the dictionary, Johnson became a prominent figure in London. At that point, the famous man whom he had wanted to meet years ago offered him a sum of money. Unhesitatingly, he returned the money, untouched. Just imagine eighteenth-century England, in which public transport was inconvenient, public libraries ill-furnished, in addition to his poverty and ill health; if Johnson had not possessed self-assurance, how could he have found the determination to engage in this great task of compiling the English dictionary? Only his unflagging confidence which had motivated him to press on, allowed him successfully to compile the dictionary, thus writing a new page in English literary history.

The phrase "my God-given talents shall be employed" teaches us that we ought to be confident. In fact, it is with self-confidence that one can both avoid self-undermining and arrogance.

Written on September 27, 1955 in early morning.

28 Empty oneself of desires and nobility follows

> *By trying our best and leaving the rest to fate, we ought to find joy in whatever work we do, and work neither for fame nor gain; only then can one cultivate a noble spirit.*

We are bound to "give" and "take" in all human interactions. The best kind of people are the ones who "give" more than they "take". To the greatest degree possible, such a person will try to smooth the way for others to the best of his ability. Confucius' notion of being "tireless in teaching" emphasises entirely this aspect of "giving". This is because the more one "gives", the more one stands to "gain".

If you were to look back on a time more than 2500 years ago, when travelling was still very inconvenient, Confucius was yet able to gather huge numbers of students when he set up his school and conducted seminars. Does this not illustrate the intangible rewards of being "tireless in teaching"?

Lao Zi was a relatively more calculating individual. He said, "Should one hope to gain, one needs first to give". The more one "gives", the more he "gains" from something. According to the aforementioned theory that "giving" more implies that one stands to "gain" more, it is more beneficial to "give' more rather than wanting to "gain" more.

The average individual strikes a better balance between "gaining" and "giving". He neither takes advantage of others, nor lets others benefit from him in any way. An exemplification would be the popular "Go Dutch" culture in European and American societies, which is more or less influenced by their principle of equal rights and obligations.

A lesser person is one who only seeks to "gain" without "giving". In his mind, he perceives himself to have profited at some other's expense, but does not realize that by adopting such an attitude, he is actually paying a price higher than that of any other person.

As the Chinese proverb goes, "Men will die for wealth, as birds will for food." This proverb reveals the disastrous consequence of human greed. If birds were not gluttonous, the chances of their getting captured would be almost zero. If people did not hanker after wealth, they would naturally be contented, leading lives that abide by conscience and simplicity. Evil would thus not exist, nor would there be an abundance of wrongdoing in the form of murder and robbery, betrayal and treason.

Dear reader, you might laugh at my conservatism but usually, in observing a person, I pay the greatest attention to his character and morality when he is out of the public eye. Only if he has a disciplined private life, never seeking easy money nor the easy way out of difficulties, will I discuss larger issues like governance and world order with him. However, should his personal life be steeped in debauchery, filled with wine, lust, avarice and pride, he cannot but go against his conscience and will end up committing all manner of unspeakable acts when he is finally unable to make ends meet.

"Asking for frost in June" is an apt expression. You have readied yourself when you have a favour to ask of others, but the other party is caught unawares. You might be eloquently persuasive, but the other party might yet not accede to your request. Indeed, it is not easy to ask a favour. Should you have to borrow money or ask a favour of an acquaintance, rather than of a close friend, I'm afraid you might hesitate to do so.

There were two men in ancient China: Qian Lou and Tao Yuanming. Qian Lou was terribly poor, but even when starving, he refused to chase for fame and honour. When a person is so determined and clear-headed, what more can one do to him? Tao Yuanming, on the other hand, refused to bend over for a living. He was resolved to be at peace with his poverty and devote himself to the spiritual. In so doing, his ideas transcended common thinking, which led him to produce great written works.

I seek not to demoralize; on the contrary, I hope to teach people to remain motivated and optimistic at all times. However, it should be stipulated that we strive to maintain a disciplined lifestyle, and not be at the mercy of the vices. By trying our best and leaving the rest to fate, we ought to find joy in whatever work we do, and work neither for fame nor gain; only then can one cultivate a noble spirit. In truth, when a person reaches the point of being devoid of desires, he will be upright, not yielding easily to others. When a person is able to stand upright, chest out, chin up, brows set, and to hold forth about all things under the sun, and is indifferent to worldly gain and loss - when a man has reached this point - need we still doubt his moral worth?

Written on 16 May 1955 at midnight

About the Translators

Dr Susan Ang

Dr Susan Ang (Ph.D., M.A., B.A. Cambridge) has taught in the Department of English Language and Literature, National University of Singapore since 1993. She specialises in Modern Poetry and teaches a wide range of subjects including modern poetry, metafictions, tragedy, science fiction and detective fiction.

Lim Zhan Yi

Lim Zhan Yi graduated with a B.A. (first class Honours) in English Literature from the National University of Singapore. He was the Editor-in-Chief of NUSMargins, the NUS Undergraduate Journal of English Literature. He is currently teaching English Language and Literature in Hwa Chong Institution.